First I Got Sober
And Then I Got Fired

First I Got Sober
And Then I Got Fired

Finding Freedom In Failure

Dan Matwey

ISBN: 978-0-9878813-0-4

To my mother for her strong example of grace and dignity amidst life's many challenges – of which she's had her share and I've certainly contributed. Her prayers and unfailing love throughout the lost years help sustain me and the encouragement and support afterwards helped restore me.

Contents

Acknowledgement

To my three children, Tim, Amber and Shae-Lynn, who have never done anything but make me proud. I can't imagine a world without them and am simply grateful I held on long enough to experience the blessing of having them in my life today.

Also, to my dear wife Sian, who throughout this writing process has always believed in me – even when I couldn't believe in myself. For the countless times she watched me looking for jobs or going off to interviews and responded with the same bold observation: "don't you dare take that job unless it's something you absolutely love. You have a book to finish – that's what you're supposed to do." And finish I did, because, and probably only because, of her loving support and encouragement.

CHAPTER 1

Familiar Words

"EXCUSE me Dan," I heard in a firm voice, glancing up to see her in the doorway. "Can you come and see me in my office?" *Oh, oh, this can't be good*, I thought. I had heard those words before and her ominous tone left me with a sense of what might come next. After all, it wasn't the first time, or even the second for that matter.

With the bank manager hovering to ensure security wasn't breached and client information stolen, I packed the box graciously handed me, cleared the office, and within minutes was on my way. *I must say, I'm getting rather efficient at this exit process*, I numbly thought while I quietly left. Of course I should be, I was getting enough practice. My instincts, a little more adept than my ability to maintain a job these days, were once again correct and off I walked into the sunset … or at least the brightness of that June afternoon. If nothing else, it was a pleasant day to be fired, which is more than can be said for the last time it happened … things were looking up.

Still shaking my head a day later and wondering when things started to go so horribly wrong, like a bolt of lightning it hit me – *I'm less employable sober, than I ever was while I was drunk.* Considering the drastic difference between those two lifestyles, it almost defied all odds. For as long as I can remember, I was allergic to alcohol. Whenever I drank I seemed to break out in spots; hospital wards, police cruisers, unfamiliar floors. I would repeatedly find myself surrounded by trouble. In contrast, the past eight were a period where I had become, if not a model citizen, than at least one who for the first time in my life gave a lot more back to society than I took from it. One might expect it would be during the former when I couldn't keep a job and the latter when I could do no wrong.

Once I was forever breaking every rule imaginable. I made it a habit to call in sick to work regularly, and motivation, commitment or aspiration couldn't have been found with a search party. Today, I had progressed to a point where I had gone back to school to earn an MBA, had upgraded my skills with every license and certification possible within my field, and was consumed by passion and vision. Strangely, I had also gone from a point where employers couldn't help but keep me to one where they couldn't wait to get rid of me. For the third time since becoming sober I had now been fired – it didn't make any sense.

What was the answer? Go back to drinking? The thought was fleeting at best, experience dictating that might not be such a good idea. Knowing what I shouldn't do was fine and good, but it didn't solve anything. Repetitive firings had rendered me clueless as to the nature of this plague with which I am seemingly afflicted – leaving me in desperate need of an answer. Maybe God was just trying to get my attention. For lack of a better explanation, that crossed my mind. Granted, this is God we're talking about, so if that were the case, surely there could have been a better way of doing so – one that still included an income would have been nice. Or at the very least something a little nobler in the way it ended, perhaps along the lines of the epiphany that sent Jerry Maguire packing – at least I could have walked away with my head held high.

The most bothersome aspect is the knowledge that today I have more to offer than ever before. At least I would think so, but evidently such sentiments aren't shared by those I have worked for since reinventing myself. With all the changes in my life these past few years, which took an inordinate amount of work and effort, the assumption was that I had arrived – ready to bear the fruit of all that hard labour. After all, it was the classic formula for success based on everything I had heard and read. Heck, having turned 50 last September, it was even my year of the proverbial jubilee and reclamation – not when I would continue to lose even more.

At my age most of my friends were pondering what they are going to do during retirement, not figuring out what they wanted to be when they grow up. It bothered me, but I found some simple reassurance in the fact that I even cared– that alone was progress. Once upon a time, nothing would have concerned me, except, perhaps a fridge with no beer in it (which would have bordered on catastrophic). Little did I care what the rest of any given day might look like, let alone what was beyond it. In many ways it was a much easier way to waltz through life – part of me would now take that feeling of indifference over disconcerting in a heartbeat. Nevertheless, I remain committed to solve this puzzle. Besides if I fail, there is always drinking to fall back on – a proven solution for making life's problems disappear.

CHAPTER 2

Responsibility isn't for Everyone

"DANNY, you've got to stop living everyday like its New Years Eve." Maybe this was when it all began, I'm not really sure. For a guy who doesn't remember an awful lot of what my mom said back in my teenage years, I vividly recall those words being spoken on a regular basis. Of course at the time I just laughed it off. I thought my mom, or for that matter anyone who felt that way, was far too uptight no matter how well intended. Why people couldn't just leave each other alone to live their own lives, I simply couldn't understand.

I liked to call myself an existentialist back then, perhaps for no other reason than because it sounded impressive. I would read books by Sartre, Kierkegaard and Camus, pretending to understand them. *I may need something to discuss at a cocktail party,* I thought (although I never had attended a cocktail party), *or a family reunion.* Others my age all seemed to have opinions to express and were extremely well spoken in doing so. I didn't want to feel left out. More than that however, what little I did comprehend about existentialism, was enough to sense its symbiotic relationship to my way of living. I could set it my own rules and do things my own way – ah what freedom. Of course, at the time I didn't have the benefit of seeing exactly where that freedom might take me. Now I know only too well.

This was all crossing my mind the day after my unceremonious departure from that job that once held such promise. I had decided to go for a stroll, trying hard to avoid feeling down on myself but knowing it was really only a matter of time before falling into a morass of self-pity. I was walking through a forest I frequented, steps away from my old house and my favorite part of the city. In the quietness, I was sure to find numerous deer along with whatever other wildlife decided to make an appearance at the time – my place to 'get away from it all'. In light of recent circumstances, there really wasn't an awful lot to get away from, except perhaps from the business that went on in my head – a region that could still get terribly congested at times. This wooded sanctuary always brought some tranquility and freedom. A far different kind of freedom than that of the existential variety I once held so dear to my heart.

As I walked that day I actually appreciated the fact that there was no need to rush out to the office that next morning. I had time to try and put things in perspective. Oddly enough, my thoughts didn't focus so much on my current situation, but rather on my early years and how I even survived, much less stay employed.

Reflecting on my mom's comments from years earlier, I couldn't help but think about my friend Ed, who in a self deprecating manner will often say, "I don't think about much, but sometimes I'm all I think about." Well, what do you know? Maybe mom was right after all, I realized. That's exactly what she had been trying to tell me all those years – I thought about nothing but myself.

There was a lot of truth to that. Responsibility was something for which I had neither the time nor the inclination (okay, maybe just not the inclination). It seemed like a lot of work that guaranteed nothing other than to impede my fun. If it was a choice between fun and something else, anything else, it really didn't matter what it was, I was always going to side with fun. Without wavering, I rode that conviction well into my adult years. It would eventually take its toll – mind you it would never get me fired.

Considering my track record it seemed like a paradox – the more irresponsible I was, the more job security I had. One former job in particular came to mind that day, which just reiterated how little sense it all made.

CHAPTER 3

What do I need to do to get fired here?

Y EARS ago, after a motorcycle accident had left me hospitalized, Nancy and I met during her time there as a student nurse. It was a lengthy stay (four months) as I underwent numerous surgeries on a severely damaged leg. I was fortunate enough to be surrounded by many quality nurses – numerous attractive ones at that. As a twenty three year old, that made an otherwise miserable experience some-what easier to bear. Nancy fell into that category and after keeping in touch after I left, we began dating and were married a few years later.

A couple of years into our marriage we decided to move to the Niagara region in 1989. That decision was based on the simple fact that houses were far more affordable there than in and around where we had been living in Toronto. She continued to commute to her job in Toronto, while I had accepted an offer for a position as a production planner with a firm closer to our new house.

A fairly large company, it employed nearly a thousand people and the plant was located in a border town. They manufactured parts, the vast majority of which were exported to the US, so their close proximity to that country made sense from a logistics standpoint.

The job itself was anything but stimulating, making it little different than previous position's I had held in a similar role as production support staff. Often so mundane in fact that other staff in my department used to wonder aloud whether or not anyone would even notice if they showed up at work. Although in my own little world most of the time and not one to pay a great deal of attention to what those around me were saying, my selective hearing was such that I didn't miss much if I thought that information would be to my benefit – that was one of those occasions.

My friend Doug was of a vastly different demeanour. Along with his gregarious nature, he was always dressed meticulously and paid great attention to detail. Although different in many ways, we were bonded by our indifference toward our job as well as our carefree attitude toward life in general.

One Sunday afternoon, having consumed numerous beverages at a local watering hole, the two of us, imagination in overdrive, were discussing that comment about nobody noticing whether or not certain office staff showed up at work. It seemed like a theory worth testing, so we concocted a plan that would do just that. If it worked, it would certainly alleviate some of that boredom that came along with our job. We would keep the idea to ourselves, sensing others couldn't be trusted to know what we had planned. There was substantial risk involved if management became aware of our scheme.

Although salaried staff, we still punched a clock upon arriving and leaving for the day. It was decided that if we merely took turns covering for one another, there would be no need for both of us to be present the entire time. After arriving for the day, one would stay at work and the other take the afternoon off, typically to go drinking – another hobby we shared. That was even more convenient given that we were a stone throw away from Buffalo where booze was a lot cheaper anyway. Since what I did at work seemed of little value anyway, my conscience wasn't the least bit shaken and I was able to rationalize that there was no harm in what we were planning. With that, the scheme was implemented and for several weeks it went off without a glitch.

"Dan, can you please come and see me in my office for a minute?" There they were again, those same words I'd later hear far too many times. On that occasion, as opposed to my job at the bank when even if it was to no avail I gave every ounce of effort to try and make a difference, this was back at that factory, when a job was simply a burden required to maintain my compromising lifestyle.

Her voice was one that couldn't be mistaken – nor forgotten, that's for sure. I never knew quite what to make of it, but would probably best describe it as being complete opposite to that of an opera singer. Whereas the singer with her unmistakable high pitch might be capable of breaking glass, I imagined that Lucy's, with its distinctive raspy tone, might very well be able to scare those broken fragments back together.

Regardless of what she sounded like, after Lucy directing me her way I figured, *that's it, the gig is up, and I'm finally busted ... oh well, it was fun while it lasted.* I continued to follow her, sauntering purposely, so as to put off the inevitable as long as possible.

"Could you do me a favour please? I'd like you to ask for a raise."

Not realizing anyone had followed us into the office, I looked behind to see who she might be talking to – surely it couldn't be me. Seeing nothing but a closed door and cracked window (which almost made me burst out laughing given what I thought her voice was capable of doing), I turned and in a dumbfounded manner mumbled something along the lines of "excuse me."

She went on to explain at length how given my job level and some of the duties involved, the union could perceive unfairness in pay between what I did compared to that of a job level higher. Basically they wanted to ensure there was no trouble, and for reasons I didn't really understand, requesting a raise would avoid any problems. After listening without trying to appear in complete shock, I simply said "okay" and was more than obliged to accommodate her request.

I walked away feeling tremendous relief, having once again

escaped the fate I knew I very well deserved. *Ah, life is so good*; there was no other way to feel at that moment. My euphoric thinking left me oblivious to the fact I was at a stage where the slope was getting increasingly slippery, while seeming that much smoother.

It seemed like a perfectly good excuse to celebrate, and after sharing the good news with Nancy that night, we did – at least I did. She on the other hand was growing increasingly concerned by that point, not quite as ecstatic as me about celebrating my good fortune.

CHAPTER 4

Get Me to the Church on Time

IT was many years later, an unusually balmy winter evening and I prepared to walk down the aisle for my second time. In terms of behaviour, I was barely recognizable as compared to that first occasion. Twenty years can do that to someone – it certainly did me.

Originally, I could have been married to the best woman in the world – even the history of the world – it really wouldn't have made a difference. I was in no position to offer anything to anybody and until I was, there wasn't the slightest hope of being in a marriage that was going to work. In all likelihood Nancy had no idea what she was getting into back then, as I was rather gifted at hiding my true nature. Of course it would only be a matter of time before it was revealed.

With the changes that had taken place, my life was different now – which impacted everything. Excluding the career related calamities, it was all for the better. After knowing Sian for a couple of years, we had decided to get married on that New Year's Eve (2010).

I adore my new wife, even though her behaviour could be described at times as, for lack of a better word, quirky. Actually, I found that aspect of her personality to be very charming when we met, although her heart for helping others is without question her most endearing quality. On top of that she is very attractive, which certainly doesn't hurt, granted, it did lead me to wonder what she possibly could have seen in me to begin with. She should be too young to be suffering from vision problems, but if her eyesight was a little deficient so be it – I wasn't about to complain. I'm just glad she isn't as perceptive as the woman at the deli counter I had encountered several years earlier.

It still makes me chuckle when I think about it all this time later. When my kids were younger, I used to be eager to do the grocery shopping at home, even if there were ulterior motives attached. While most men's favorite past time while off running errands might include browsing through a hardware store fondly looking at power tools, I was far more comfortable strolling through the aisles of a supermarket. While en route to do so it also gave me ample opportunity to stack up on supplies from the liquor store, which I could easily conceal amongst the bags of groceries I brought home. Such errands typically involved one or more of my kids, as was the case that particular evening while out with my eldest daughter Amber. She would have been about six months old at the time. There is something about carting a baby around a grocery store that will cause women (which may also have been a motivating factor for doing the shopping) to stop in their tracks and comment at length about how cute he or she is. That is true pretty well anywhere you find a woman and baby in the same vicinity, which I've never quite been able to understand. Actually, I find ugly kids far more interesting to look at, if only because they are far rarer to see. I always loved a Winston Churchill comment I recalled hearing years ago. When seeing a particularly unattractive infant he was known to say "now that's a baby."

I didn't get any of those comments with my daughter, just an ongoing supply of affectionate observers. On this occasion, waiting at the back of the store lined up in the Deli section, it was an elderly woman who initiated the conversation. With her distinguished white hair resting on a delicate fur coat and piercing eyes that penetrated dark bifocals, there was something about her that her that wasn't easily ignored. I can still recall the commanding tone to her voice.

For ten minutes she went on about how cute my daughter was and I was beginning to wonder if she would ever leave, when finally her husband appeared and it was clear she was ready to go. She took a lengthy look at my daughter one last time and after commenting on how beautiful Amber was, she quickly looked at me once more, as if something weren't right. Staring me straight in the eyes without flinching she said, "You must have an awfully pretty wife" – and away she went.

So yeah, either love is blind, or Sian's eyesight isn't all it's cracked up to be. I'm just glad my eyes work well, it makes her presence that much more enjoyable.

"So, where do you think we should go for dinner dear?" After asking, she went on to request it be somewhere that we wouldn't be overly rushed. Then added "And not too spicy" – which in my opinion is the only downfall about marrying a Welsh girl. I can't for the life of me understand how the British can enjoy such bland food.

It was exactly six months since we had been married and we wanted to do something special for the evening. It was also two weeks since being fired from my most recent job; there was still plenty to be discussed about that event and what our future might hold.

Sian and I had met at a church related singles group a few years ago, well after my last drink and whenever stories from the past did come to the surface, she had always figured it was somewhat of an embellishment on my part to try and spice things up a bit. She had never seen me drink. She found it hard to even imagine me as an alcoholic, but had she been around to witness it, would be entirely aware of the fact that there was little need to spice up anything – tone it down a bit, maybe. Always the inquisitive type regardless of who she was talking to, and being one who loved to hear details, she was forever asking questions about my past. It didn't matter what it was, jobs, school, women, etc – Sian didn't hesitate to ask.

Unlike most men, I wasn't one particularly enamoured with the fairer sex during my teenage years, which was something she found difficult to believe – given what most teenage boys are prone to be like. To some extent it may have been a result of attending an all male high school and lacking the same exposure to girls as most guys my age – but I knew there was more to it than that. And it certainly wasn't because I wasn't attracted to women – years later, without having drinking to turn to, that almost became a problem of its own. So, upon her asking one of those inquisitive 'don't spare the details' questions that evening, I went on to explain.

CHAPTER 5

I Can't Dance

I was sharing a story about my high school days, in particular a hockey tournament that I attended while in grade ten. St Mike's is a well known Catholic high school in Toronto – probably as famous for the hockey players it's produced over the decades as much as anything else. Back in the days when I attended in the 1970's if you went to St Mike's it seemed you were either Italian, or played hockey.

That year our Bantam team was travelling to Drummondville Quebec for a tournament. It was quite prestigious amongst our age group, attracting many quality teams from all over the country, and even abroad. Practically all I knew about Drummondville at the time was that there was a hockey stick named after the town, and that they sold Brador – considerably stronger beer than what you could buy in Ontario. The train ride was a lengthy one (although likely not nearly as long as those unfortunate enough to be on the same car), but we were pretty excited to reach our destination. For most, it was the first time away from our parents for any considerable length of time.

Shortly after arriving, we were to learn that a couple of what we figured to be long standing myths about Quebec was in fact quite true. For one, it was bitterly cold with several feet of snow on the ground – there had been no exaggeration about the weather. This remote town lived up to everything we had ever heard about winter in the province of Quebec.

That wasn't what got our attention though – there was a greater truth much more exciting to discover. Barely off the train and having a chance to get settled, it had soon become clear that we had stumbled upon paradise – a countless exhibition of cute girls surrounded us. Really, really cute girls that is, like those adorable French girls we had always heard about and assumed had been vastly overstated. Their presence alone would have made the train ride worth it.

I'm not sure if it was the girls in attendance that threw us off our game or the fact we really weren't blessed with an abundance of talent to begin with – we failed pretty miserably in the tournament that week. It was an entirely different result with the young ladies though, or so I was told, there would be no opportunity to have any firsthand knowledge.

Our first night there, the team had been invited to a dance at the local high school, which for a bunch of hormone crazed 15 year olds from an all guy high school, was pretty much like winning the lottery. On the way, a few of us ducked into 'Ye Old Taverne', a small inconspicuous looking pub, with old stone stairs leading underground. I can still picture the dimly lit sign and narrow entrance. The fact we were a group 15 year olds who were well under-age wasn't even an issue – this was Quebec in the mid seventies and no fake identification was necessary. Three of the guys left within minutes and continued on to the dance, but my friend Mickey and I stayed for the night. We sat with a boisterous group of old (or so they seemed, but were more likely my age now) Frenchman who loved the fact we were from St Mikes. In broken English they spoke with enthused fondness of Frank Mahovolich, Gerry Cheevers, Tim Horton, Davey Keon and many others. Beer and stories just kept on coming and I had never felt so at home in my life – I experienced something exhilarating that evening.

We heard the next morning from our teammates about the amazing time we had missed, with many stories (fabricated as they may have been they were still fun to listen to) of intimate encounters. My absence was never questioned, but the two of us were strongly encouraged to take part that next evening when there would be another dance. Life doesn't always offer such a reprieve.

The routine that next day would be very similar to the one prior, falling victim once more in a very one-sided decision on the ice. It wasn't overly demoralizing to the guys – in fact it was forgotten almost immediately. The really important stuff was just about to get started. There would be other hockey games (although not in this tournament, we had made a quick exit), but certainly never again the chance to spend an evening in the presence of so many beautiful young ladies.

So once again off we went to the dance, even Mickey this time, but not me. Walking through the streets, I had slipped through to the back unnoticed, in a manner so habitual it would have made Pavlov's dog appear impetuous. I didn't even think about it, simply taking the detour and finding myself back at the same bar.

With the thrill of the evening before still fresh in my mind, I took a seat and felt right at home. I couldn't have imagined anywhere else I would rather be, even two blocks away drooling over the prettiest girls I had ever seen. Same guys, same chairs, they sat, they drank, and they reminisced about the good old days. I was fifteen years old, yet I joyfully sat there reminiscing – about what?

The fact is, as I went on to explain to Sian that evening, from a very young age, even given the most attractive option possible, I would side with alcohol every time. From a woman who had never in her life used any substance, alcohol or otherwise, to alter her state of mind, she simply could not understand why I would allow myself to miss out on so much. What could possibly have motivated me?

From the outside looking in, I had to admit that it didn't make an awful lot of sense and although I didn't have all the answers, I sure had a pretty good idea where it all started. Perhaps it was for no other reason than the fact I was so well mentored.

CHAPTER 6

A Family Tradition

"MR. Matwey, I can drive if you like." Although somewhat an unreasonable request from a thirteen year old, those words were pleasing to my ears at the time. Shawn was never shy about saying what was on his mind. A close friend since kindergarten, he was tall and lanky, looking much older than his age. He was a regular fixture at our house, coming in unannounced and making himself comfortable if nobody was around to greet him – a standard policy of my parents for any friend. Along with my dad, we were driving Shawn home after he had spent the day at our place.

It was a typical summer day, at least what it used to be before technology kept a kid indoors to the degree it does today. We occupied our time riding 5 speed bikes, playing lacrosse with whatever neighbourhood kids could be rounded up, and eating everything in sight as we sporadically stormed into the kitchen.

Shortly after getting in the car to leave, I came to that familiar realization of what my father had been up to since coming home from work a few hours earlier. I was always too scared to go in and check, afraid of what I might find. I had seen him in pretty bad shape before, many times in fact, but none quite like this.

We were barely teenagers at the time and as only childhood buddies who know everything about each other would, I was aware that Shawn had practiced driving with older relatives. That was reassuring because as embarrassing as that moment was (and there would be many more), him taking over behind the wheel couldn't be any worse than the alternative. Within a couple of minutes my dad was asleep in the passenger seat as Shawn drove the rest of the way to his house, having the presence of mind to stop a block or so away instead of pulling into his driveway. The stupor was short lived and my dad was then able to get us home. How in the world this went unnoticed to the police or others on the road and my dad managed to avoid the consequences he deserved either that or most other days, still remains a mystery.

Not that it seemed appalling at the time, in fact I was used to it and besides, he did a lot of good things while sober. My father was quite generous with his time and very popular with my friends. He could tell a great story and had the ability to genuinely speak to kids at their own level – they considered him genuine. He spent countless hours helping coach sports teams and was often carting kids back and forth to various games. He also worked plenty of extra hours to support our activities. Along with my mom, he was involved in numerous groups and spent a lot of time entertaining. I very much admired him in many ways, particularly his ability to be so outgoing and easily converse with everyone – quite opposite to the shyness I possessed. Some of his stories were legendary, having been extremely popular in his younger years.

Notwithstanding the predicament of that moment, as a kid I was actually quite happy and well adjusted. I played competitive sports year round and had many close friends. I had a brother and sister I looked up to and loving parents who I now understand had tried their best. My mom is quite intelligent and it wasn't until years later that I realized the sacrifices she had made. Coming from a family of little means, post secondary schooling wasn't an option after being an outstanding high school student. She fell into a career as a secretary at a large firm with their head office across the street from our house. She was likely more capable than most of her managers – yet held no bitterness. Like many parents of her generation, she just wanted her children to have a better future than that which she was denied. My father's drinking began to take its toll though and theirs was a marriage headed for trouble.

That was a dark side I didn't understand, but simply accepted as coming with the territory. There were kids who had it much worse off, so I shouldn't complain. At the same time, I did wonder why he wouldn't just smarten up and stop drinking so much. It should be simple enough – or so I thought. Little did I know I too was defective to the point that I was born without a stop button.

Many times I found his behaviour so repulsive that I swore I would never act in the manner he had. Yet years later, there I was displaying those same unconscionable and unexplainable acts around my own kids and others – except that I wasn't going to escape the negative consequences. I had heard the term 'generational curse' before, even as a kid before ever having had a drink. I really didn't give the concept too much consideration – maybe I should have.

The evidence was there to support it, a family of origin with a history of abusing alcohol. Not only was my father an alcoholic, my grandfather and his father before him were as well. Was that the reason I would go on to drink the way I did? It likely didn't hinder the process, but it also provided a convenient excuse, a form of self-deception to justify my behaviour. That was immensely easier than trying to change.

Whether or not there was a 'generational curse' at work in passing along an addiction is an argument I thought best left for others to intellectualize over. I would have balked at the whole idea anyhow. A genetic disposition to do what I liked to do best – to drink – how could anyone even consider that as a curse? If anything, I would have called it a blessing.

Anybody who has spent even the even slightest bit of time with someone active in any addiction would know all about excuses, having heard them a million times until they sound like a broken record. I was no different and could rationalize (not that much of it was rational) just about anything, conveniently helping avoid any guilt that might accompany my poor choices.

I played that family history card many, many times. So much so in fact, years later it was fairly easy to see right through anyone trying to do the same thing and I would be more than happy to call them on it. If I knew then what I did now, would I have acted differently? Not likely, but after being particularly intrigued by a show I happened to watch one evening, I wondered if that might have had an impact.

CHAPTER 7

Paralysis by Omission

SOME of the shows I've become accustomed to watching on TV the past few years are vastly different than what once would have projected from the screen. 'Life Today', hosted by James and Betty Robinson, would fall into that category. Beth Moore is a fairly well known teacher and speaker in Christian circles, she is also a regular guest on that show and a woman I love listening to whenever I get the chance. I find her talks very inspiring, offering unique insight and this particular lesson included a story I wouldn't soon forget.[1]

It isn't without some degree of discomfort that I watch her speak, because it is quite clear that Beth always talks to a captivated audience of about 150 women – seldom a man in site. *Oh no*, I remember thinking while watching one evening, *maybe there was something to that revelation that occurred a month or two prior.*

That evening I was at the office trying to make phone calls to prospective clients in an effort to drum up business as a self employed Financial Consultant at the time. I had about the same enthusiasm for making cold calls as I did as a ten year old when my mom took me to what was then the O'Keefe Center in Toronto to watch the ballet 'Nutcracker Suite' – nothing short of painful I remember. At any rate, based on the success I was having on the phone that evening, my lack of enthusiasm was no doubt transparent to anyone

---

1 Beth Moore *Life Today with James and Betty Robinson* CTS June 2008.

DAN MATWEY

on the other end of the line as well. I'd had enough, so the idea came to call a friend and see if she wanted to go to a movie.

Deb lived in a small town not far north or me, an older picturesque community surrounded by natural beauty. It was well matched to her personality, she being very conscientious and passionate about sustainable development and harmony with nature. We had met at a meditation workshop a year or two earlier and remained in close contact.

Her community also happened to have one of those old style movie theatres of the variety you seldom find anymore in the world of modern multi faceted mega theatres. I asked if there were any decent movies on that night and she replied that the only thing playing was 'Jane Austin Book Club'. Sure I figured, why not. Not that I had heard of it, but that also meant I hadn't heard anything bad, so it was worth a shot.

With my work night done, I hurried to pick her up and we entered a couple of minutes into the previews, stumbling through the darkness trying not to step on anybody while finding a seat. I was lost in the world of fantasy, far removed from problems of my own, eating popcorn and thoroughly enjoying myself – I was quite pleased with my decision to bail on work obligations. Then it happened, as the lights to the theatre came on, I was moments away from turning beat red. Not so much because of the shock that came with observing a theatre that included aside from me, 21 women and not a male in sight, rather from the realization that I probably enjoyed the show more than anyone else in attendance. And then it hit me – oh my God I like chic flicks.

That was part of the price to be paid for trading the emotionless, numbing existence of life with alcohol to one where years of suppressed feelings were allowed to come to the surface. I also now realized why it was for the past couple of years I could never seem to watch 'Touched by an Angel' without crying. *I'm such a basket case*, I thought. So, I could only laugh from the point forward whenever

I watched Beth and it seemed to be just me and the girls – it wasn't about to stop me.

In this particular story that she was relaying at the time, it involved Gilda Radnor, my favorite cast member back when I watched Saturday Night Live years earlier. Many would remember her Rosanne Rossannadanna character; she was a very funny woman who unfortunately died of cancer at far too young of an age. It revolved around an event from Gilda's childhood years at home. She was referring to her days as a kid and their family dog was expecting a litter of puppies. Along with the rest of her family she was extremely excited, looking with anticipation to the day it would happen.

One afternoon the dog was involved in an accident, whereby she crossed paths with a riding mower in their backyard. It was very serious and both its hind legs were severed at the top. They rushed the dog to the veterinarian in the hope that the puppies could be salvaged, however were advised it was far too premature for any to be expected to survive. What could be done however was that the dog could have its wounds closed and sewn? Effectively, it would learn to walk on its front legs, while dragging its rear portion behind. So, having no real choice, that's exactly what they choose to do. Shortly thereafter, her dog gave birth to eight perfectly healthy puppies – all of which walked just like their mom.

For me, that story is a perfect illustration of what I was capable of changing, yet choose not to. My continued behaviour had nothing to do with my family origin and everything to do with using it as an excuse. It's a story I especially like to share with younger addicts in recovery, those who like me might be setting themselves up to use the 'genetic disposition' excuse for years to come.

There's something about feeling invincible at a young age, without having the slightest idea of the precarious circumstances addictive behaviour presents. There's always a sense that regardless of whether or not a problem exists, it's something that can be addressed another day – one that may never arrive. A story I can tell only because I'm one of the lucky ones.

Today it frustrates me to no end to see others adopt the attitude I had. Like them I embraced the excuse when I was their age. Why wouldn't I? It was my license to drink, one which was exercised quite liberally.

CHAPTER 8

First Job – Setting a Precedent

AT a young age alcohol already had a strong grip on my mind, which should have been evident after that hockey tournament in grade ten. Over the next few years it proved to become a permanent fixture in my lifestyle. Without having finished high school, it had already become not only a favorite pastime socially, but would set a precedent for my working life.

"Hi Danny, it's your favorite aunt calling. We were thinking it might be a good idea to come and work out here for the summer. It would be great for your cousins to have you around."

In spite of the fact that she always found it necessary to remind me, she really was among my favorite Aunt's. Marie was my dad's younger sister; as such she had firsthand knowledge of his lifestyle and the problem's that went along with it – perhaps she was trying to rescue me from a similar fate. She was a very generous woman, with quick sense of humor, always wanting to know what was new in my life. It seemed like a great idea, I really didn't have a lot going on during the summer after Grade 11 anyway. Besides, it would be great to spend some time with my cousins.

They lived in a small town near Lake Erie, far enough that I considered it to be an adventure far superior to the option of spending a boring summer at home. My uncle was a tall, very distinguished looking man who had experienced his own share of hardships throughout his life. Very well read and exceptionally bright, unlike his outgoing wife, he was far more reserved by nature. He worked as a manager for the municipality and offered me a position with the city parks and cemetery crew. With plenty of physical labour in the form of cutting grass and digging foundations for gravestones, it would be a great way to keep in shape for the upcoming hockey season. Plus, I looked at it as an opportunity to make a little extra money and have some fun out of town that summer.

My aunt was especially looking forward to my stay, in the hope that I could help play the role of mentor and a big brother to my younger cousins. All three were tall good-looking lads (which would cause many to doubt I was even related) and very gifted athletes. Rob, Scott and Mike were only separated by a few years in age and had a prodigious ability to find something to fight about (actually it was more like engaging in war), before the sun went down on any given day. I've still never seen anything quite like it. The only thing worse than trying to get between them, was to get on the wrong side of any one of the three. It really didn't matter which it was, that's the only time they united for a common cause and from what I witnessed it generally didn't work out too well for the perpetrator.

For the most part though, they were good kids, although I didn't see why my presence for a few months would be of benefit. However, I wasn't going to argue with my aunt and graciously accepted their hospitality and agreed to spend the summer. Little did she realize that having me try and act as role model to her kids would be about as useful as placing one's trust in and asking the ringleader of a ponzi scheme to handle one's finances.

It would be the first of many, many times in my life that someone would go out of their way to accommodate me and I would show my gratitude in the least appropriate way possible. In this case by instilling the worst of all possible habits in kids at that impressionable age where they were most vulnerable. Underage myself and not legally in a position to buy alcohol, my cousins and their friends were even further removed from that privilege – I saw no reason for that to prevent it from being available for our consumption. I had never been one for rules, or anything that inhibited the fun desired. Regardless of whether I was a guest or not, that certainly wasn't about to change.

My first act of 'mentoring' consisted of smuggling beer onto our worksite the night in advance so we had something to enjoy while working unsupervised the next day. It wasn't to be found in my job description, but I thought it was an excellent idea – good for employee morale. Under the work conditions that summer it was very easily done and happened frequently. One of the managers would often take our crew and drop us off; returning several hours later after attending to other matters. Too much time in the sun would typically suffice as an excuse if one or two looked a little worse for wear upon being picked up.

On other days, rain would be falling in the morning, forcing us to delay getting started. For me that was merely an invitation to do something a little more exciting – most of these young teens were introduced to the idea of road trips through my prompting. In those days it wasn't difficult to get a case from the beer store and leaving it accessible in the back seat was a common practice – at least it was for me and my friends. For kids that young though, this was their first exposure to such conduct – they found it thrilling. It helped me achieve instant popularity, which was something I desperately craved. That I would introduce them to such behaviour, thereby setting a precedent for their own irresponsible choices for years to come, would be just one more part of the shame to be shed at a later date.

As the sun shone brightly later in the day, with work to be done and me nowhere in sight or returning any time soon, that was my contribution towards teaching them how to become responsible and dependable employees. If that sense of entitlement and 'everyday is New Years Eve' mentality was good enough for me,

I figured it only made sense to teach those who would listen to adopt the same self centered standards – they would likely thank me for it later.

If that wasn't enough, much to my aunt and uncle's chagrin, I didn't exactly leave the best impression around the small community either. Aside from my shenanigans at the various hotel pubs throughout that summer, it was never more evident than my final weekend there. Not that I had intended it that way, but like so many other times in my life, I had set out for an innocent evening of fun, only to see it end by being the centre of attention – generally for all the wrong reasons.

As it does on an annual basis, Dunnville was hosting its Mudcat Festival that weekend. An event that's title is derived from the fish most commonly found in the Grand River flowing through the town before exiting into Lake Erie; almost every resident of the community would be present that Saturday night. In the local arena, surrounded by pubs and beer tents that overflowed the previous few days, there was always a large dance to wrap things up.

I had disappeared a little early from the house, not waiting for my oldest cousin and his friends as planned. Conspicuous by my absence, it was assumed they would catch up with me at some point, proceeding as a group. Making their way downtown, "you've got to be kidding" were the only words that could be heard from Rob's mouth. Rounding a corner, from blocks away they looked to see a silhouette against the starry evening sky – it could only be one person.

The carnival portion of the evening was long over, with all booths abandoned and all rides shut down with lights off, except for one – the Ferris wheel. There, seated on the circular structure was one single rider, who had given the operator just enough beer to coax him into letting him go for one final ride. I remembered refusing to get off after that, but couldn't recall exactly what prompted the man to leave me at the top with the ride stopped. It wouldn't be the first time I had provoked someone to react in an unorthodox manner. In disbelief, or at least moderate surprise (nothing I did surprised too many people), my friends quickly hurried there. They convinced the operator to let me off with the assurance I wouldn't return. No harm done I figured and we ventured toward the arena in anticipation of an evening of fun. Depending on just what one's idea of fun might be, what transpired next may or may not qualify.

My recollection left a bit to be desired that night, but those nearby wouldn't suffer from a similar form of amnesia. I had never been considered much of a dancer; as a matter of fact I was downright horrible. Maybe it's because of my days at an all guy high school electing to drink beer and play shuffle board rather than attend a dance at St Josephs, Loreto Abby, or any of the nearby girl's schools that hosted dances on a regular basis. Or maybe I just had two left feet – either way, I was bad. After a couple of beers though, my inhibitions eventually vanished and although I may not have considered myself Fred Astaire reincarnated, I figured I wasn't chopped liver either.

Feeling the urge, it seemed like a good night to dance. The only question that remained was who would be lucky (or crazy) enough to join me. There she was, I had spotted her sixty feet away. With an enthusiasm that couldn't be contained, she was little different than the type I would typically ask on those rare occasions I would dance. It was clear her degree of sobriety at the time paralleled my own, so although unlikely candidates for a spot dance prize, we were well suited for one another. What I lacked in talent, she more than made up for in experience. At seventy some odd years, she certainly had a few more dances in her than I did in my seventeen. We were doing well, or at least we were having fun and I thought we were doing well, but trouble was on the horizon.

As the 'chicken dance' played, that irritating tune from the seventies that can still be heard at some weddings, it was an achievement to stay on our feet. Though we somehow envisioned ourselves as gracefully waltzing, it wasn't nearly to the extent that her husband waltzed across the floor to confront me He had me within his range and was set to teach me a thing or two for stealing his girl, only to retreat briefly, extricating and placing his dentures on the table. Unknown to me, between the three of us, we were beginning to attract a bit of attention. Now ready to reclaim his woman, he came charging uninterrupted with one arm wildly swinging towards me. At the same time he began shouting at me with a pronounced lisp, while I had enough sense to exit and escape unscathed. Nobody watching will have forgotten the sight that night when I faced the wrath of the most unlikely of bullies – a toothless geriatric with a speech impediment.

A summer that began by holding so much promise, ultimately ended with being a series of one deplorable episode after another. At the time, I could easily laugh it off. As the pattern continued in the years that followed, it gradually turned into a way of living one would commonly associate with the pathetic representation of an alcoholic – I was having too much fun to see it.

With nothing to be learned from my behaviour and few consequences as a result from my actions, it seemed to be a pretty good formula for success – an even better one for failure. I saw no reason to change, so I didn't. Throughout that summer and years to follow, this was a portrait of the guy that people not only wanted to employ, but refused to fire. Thinking about it now, years later, I was as perplexed as ever.

CHAPTER 9

So Close Yet so Far

I had been about an hour walking in the woods before I finally came across some familiar friends, with my first deer sighting of the day. There was a group four, including two that were babies not much larger than the size of a dog. Other than a quick glance, they didn't let my presence interrupt whatever snack they had found on the forest floor. I loved this place.

What a difference between then and now, today able to enjoy nature and finding something spiritual about the quiet surroundings. I was able to fully appreciate so many elements of creation that surrounded me – this had become my place to connect with God.

I could only shake my head as I considered what I had missed throughout the years. Many times amongst the most magnificent sights the world had to offer, yet completely oblivious to the beauty around me. I thought about the places I had been when the obsession to drink trumped everything else, and imagined what it might be like to revisit them today.

As a kid I always dreamt of what it might be like to see the Rocky Mountains. While watching TV and seeing the Alps during events like a world cup downhill race in Garmisch-Partenkirchen (my all time favorite name for a city), I would pride myself in the fact that I lived in a country with mountains equally as majestic – better perhaps.

I finally did have the chance while visiting Banff and Jasper in the mid 80's. A year earlier, Nancy and I had borrowed some money for a small down payment towards the purchase a rental property in Calgary. With a depressed market and the cyclical nature of a region dependent upon a commodity like oil, it seemed like good long-term investment. With relatives in Calgary I thought it would be nice to visit, perhaps popping by to take a look at our investment in the process. Despite the city's confusing street pattern we finally found it and spent about five seconds looking at the first house we had ever purchased. "There it is, that's nice", that was the extent of the communication. We were never to see the house again and certainly wouldn't make any money from it.

If I ever want to consider what the financial impact of what my addiction might have been, this would be a good place to start. We sold that house two years later for virtually the same price we paid for it. Had we held it for the long-term investment it was originally intended, twenty years later when Calgary had become a hot bed for Canadian real estate, we could have realized a phenomenal return on that investment – but I was running out of drinking money. With no kids and both of us having full time jobs along with very little debt and marginal housing costs, I still couldn't afford to support my lifestyle.

I did see the Rockies that year and even though I was surrounded by sensational mountain peaks and glaciers, my greatest pleasure came when we stopped for drinks and I was staring at the walls of a pub. That's where I spent as much time as possible during that vacation and I may as well have been in the Burlington Bay with the mountain (as the folks from Hamilton like to refer to the Niagara escarpment) as a backdrop – it would have made little difference and been a lot less expensive.

There were many other occasions that were wasted due to my incessant need to stop for a drink. In Quebec City, which I believe is about as spectacular as it gets in Canada if looking to experience a European flavour, I couldn't get past the first outside patio I found.

Spending the entire afternoon and evening, I never came close to exploring the city as was planned while stopping over returning from a lacrosse tournament. Sure, the girls were cute, but I already knew that from my Drummondville experience years earlier. The brick streets, the brilliant architecture and amazing view of the St Lawrence from those forts that once held intruders at bay – those would be left to be seen on TV when I got home. At the time they were a ten minute walk away.

The most ridiculous of all was during a trip to the United Arab Emirates just prior to the Gulf war. My stepfather, who taught at a local college outside of Toronto, was teaching there on a two-year contract and my mom had invited Nancy and me over for the Christmas holidays. It was quite beautiful really and if I ever desired to gain an appreciation for the diversity of what nature had to offer, this would be the ultimate place to find it. Within a three hour period we could go from seeing the beaches of the Persian gulf (near Dubai where we were staying), journey along with the camels across the awe inspiring deserts with their shifting sand dunes, and ultimately reach a point bordering Oman where snow was visible on the mountaintops.

There are places in my country where in the same period of time I could ride for hours and when finished, find myself in a place with no discernable difference in appearance than when I had started.

So with an opportunity of a lifetime and the chance to behold what had to be amongst nature's greatest treasures, what did I enjoy most about the trip? Unequivocally it would be happy hour in downtown Dubai. I had travelled half way across the globe, to an Arab land far removed from Western civilization. The most exciting aspect was that I had surprisingly found myself to be in the one remote region of the Middle East in which alcohol was legal – most of that holiday may as well have been spent in downtown Toronto.

I remember once hearing a phrase (attributed to CS Lewis I believe) stating that "the notion of man chasing God is as ludicrous a thought as that of a mouse chasing a cat". Chasing is something I can stop doing today that I was once never capable of – not even enough to stop and appreciate what was around me. I didn't know how to slow down, let alone stop – today I can do that and enjoy the quiet. If I ever want to connect with God these days I'm acutely aware of the fact that I first need to stop – absolutely everything.

I'm still amazed to think that I no longer find it necessary to have a drink, given the fact that once upon a time, no matter what I did to try and stop, inevitably I would find myself drunk by the end of the day – whether I wanted to or not. It ruined not only vacations; it ruined a lot of things.

It wasn't always like that and I'm not really sure when that line was crossed and I lost control. At some point I did and afterwards there was no turning back. If my university days weren't when it happened, they sure weren't one for developing any academic skills either. At a time when most people left behind their teenage tendencies and began to evolve into the adults they were designed to become, mine was none other than a breeding ground for the addictive life that lay ahead.

CHAPTER 10

Higher Education – for all the Wrong Reasons

FOR many students, as fun as high school was, it included learning a bit about discipline and afterwards college or university was the period when it was balanced with responsibility, helping mature into a well rounded adult. I was late getting started, but assumed it would be no different for me, even though I did little to warrant being accepted into university. Given my haphazard approach to high school, my grades were nothing to write home about – let alone take home. I simply attributed it to a lack of ability on my part, since most of my friends had their share of fun as well, yet managed to do quite well academically.

At age 42 when I began working on an MBA, in spite of my fear of failure, I committed to actually doing the work and to my astonishment saw A's for the first time in my life. For all those years I was under the misconception those guys back in high school were that much smarter than me. What they had actually done was work a lot harder. After putting in an honest effort for the first time in my life, I was rewarded for it. I only wish it didn't take me 30 years longer than everyone else to figure that out – no wonder I still don't know what I want to be when I grow up.

In my first go around at post secondary education, the only possible way of getting accepted was to apply to a school not overly stringent about grades. I settled on one that didn't have the highest of academic standards and would accept just about anybody.

"Hey Dan, you should give Trent some thought. It looks like a great spot". My best buddy Mac suggested I join him for a weekend visit to check things out. Very laid back and down to earth by nature, he wasn't caught up in any of the prestige or hype attached to many other schools – he was simply looking for enjoyable experience. Another high school friend, Mike, would be attending as well. He didn't quite share Mac's quiet demeanour, prone to unpredictable behaviour, which could be a little frightening for opponents on the ice. Both were guys of integrity – I thought it might rub off on me. We had played hockey together through high school and also spent time together drinking and sharing our deepest thoughts. Both of them were bright enough to get accepted elsewhere, I was just glad they opted for the one spot that would take me.

My parents had recently divorced when I started my first year, which was fortuitous as I saw it. The government's system for aiding students benefited those from broken homes, receiving far more money in terms of grants than in loans – it's the only reason I applied. It had nothing to do with academics; rather the excessive handouts to fund a lifestyle that would be a lot easier than working. I had no real desire to pay back even the small amount I did receive through loans, nor would I have much of a capacity to do so for a lengthy period of time. While my friends struggled with part time jobs and worked hard to fund their way through school, I once again managed to avoid any responsibility and things worked out fine just the same – that's how I thought life worked.

The courses were manageable as well; that first year I choose a timetable that would offer the least class time at fourteen hours per week. It's a workload that I still struggled to meet. So farcical was my degree of seriousness, it included a fortnightly tutorial in both an Anthropology and Philosophy course scheduled at the same time on a Wednesday afternoon. Not wanting to show any favourtism,

I did the only thing I thought to be fair – attending neither. That's the type of effort I put in.

My next few years were little different, continuing with school for no other reason than to play hockey and go to pubs. I dated Sue for a while, becoming the envy of a lot of other guys in that residence. She was exceptionally bright, extremely cute and delightfully witty. She might have been just the thing to straighten out a guy like me, who was long overdue to correct his path, but there were one of two routes I had the choice to explore and I chose the one that didn't include her. I remained completely void of any other ambitions or desires whatsoever, concealing my admiration for those who seemed to walk through life with some sense of purpose. I often wondered what that must have felt like.

If courses became too hard I would simply drop them, setting the stage for a continuing pattern in life whereby I would quit whatever became too difficult. Eventually I would spare myself the agony and not bother trying in the first place. As much as excessive drinking was part of the school culture, particularly in residence where I stayed, most learned how to balance it with their studies. Those were the life skills and lessons others experienced in setting a foundation for a pursuit of their goals, whereas I was headed down a completely different path – one with an ending that appeared to be dismal.

I'd even abandoned those things that previously helped develop and maintain character. Church and religion had become a thing of the past and I would surround myself with others who felt the same way – it made my lifestyle easier to live with. These were students on an intellectual pursuit which included the need to question the very rules which had been designed to suppress their freedom, creativity and ability to think. Passionate about being liberated from the dogmatic traditions of the past, I thought the arguments to support it were better left to them – I just wanted to buy into the outcome.

The only aspect of those rebellious arguments that did bother me was some of the criticism I would hear being voiced against the church. Rumblings of abuse had fairly recently begun to be pronounced and was being voiced with greater volume and regularity. What were once well-concealed secrets from decades gone by were finally being allowed to surface. I could certainly understand where their anger and sense of betrayal would have come from for those who had been affected. Had it been me, I would have felt the same way. There had to be a tremendous degree of pain for both the victims and their families, and the abuse initiated by men in such a position of power and trust was inexcusable. However the fact that all priests were seemingly implicated as if all cut from the same cloth troubled me.

I had never forgotten, or lost respect for the priests who taught at St Mikes – there were some extremely good men who had sacrificed plenty to carry out their vocation. It bothered me that they might be judged negatively simply by their association with those who did abuse their roles.

Something about it didn't seem fair, although perhaps it was simply a hidden sense of guilt. Those men had to live with that stigma, having had done nothing to deserve it, while my selfish lifestyle wreaked havoc without having to pay the price I should. For many years, that's about as close as I would ever get to having empathy for anyone.

I didn't have time to be concerned for anyone else, my world now revolved around meeting my own needs – it wasn't healthy. I could see it, and I could feel it, about the only thing I couldn't do was something about it. Even my friends were beginning to comment on my excessive drinking, something which I just chose to ignore. My need to remain in denial over what had clearly become a problem began early and took on many forms.

My years at university were the only time that I ever remained committed to doing so, but I would stop drinking during lent.

Drawing from a routine regularly practiced as a result of my upbringing, ostensibly it was a done as an expression of my Catholic faith. In reality, it was merely an effort to be convinced that I couldn't possibly have a drinking problem. *Really*, I would think, *if someone could abstain for forty days, how could they be an alcoholic*? So I tried and succeeded– it was just the other 325 that were a problem.

After another couple of years at that small school, I came to the conclusion it wasn't the healthiest of environments. Aside from the alcohol, drugs were prevalent and I thought it might do me well to be in real school with serious students. There were actually plenty where I was, I just wouldn't know where to find them. The library for example – a building I might see only in passing. Although I didn't learn much through my studies, I did develop some survival skills and it became engrained in my thinking that whenever an aspect of my life would get out of control, something or someone must always have been the reason for it. In that case it was the school.

So I moved to a new one, leaving behind an army of folks who were a bad influence. Firmly planted in a new environment all would be right with the world – a tactic I've since heard referred to as a 'geographic cure'. However, as I was to find out again and again over the next few decades, every time I moved I always took the biggest problem along – myself.

Waterloo University was an hour or so west of Toronto. This move would quiet all my naysayers, and I would go and find the success I was destined for. It would also leave those problems where they belonged – in the past and in a region far way.

Outside of Munich, Germany, the largest Bavarian festival in the world takes place in the Kitchener/Waterloo region where I had relocated, with things getting under way in mid October. Sure, great music and food as part of the festivities, but to a large extent it's a week that's renowned for its excessive drinking. It draws tremendous crowds to partake in the fun and likely the only thing that comes close to the sale of beer in the region that week would be the purchase of tablets – those that would relieve a hangover as opposed to the hand held device.

There I was, barely a month into my new life, at a new school with a new found resolve to change my ways. Douger was another high school friend who went to the same school. Aside from peculiar math when filling out a scorecard while golfing, he was pretty astute academically. We had a lot fun together during high school as well; a friendship developed spending time at various bars throughout the city. He had a serious side that kicked in when the limits were pushed and pretty responsible which translated into success as a student – perhaps I was just a late bloomer.

With him and some new acquaintances from school, I was attending one of those aforementioned Oktoberfest events. People had been talking about it for weeks, an evening I looked forward to with great anticipation. It was to be my moment of redemption, presenting to the world a new and improved version of myself – I was denied entry for being too drunk. For many who attend, this is an event for which the entire point is to become as intoxicated as possible, yet I had gone so far I wasn't even allowed in. This grand plan of mine wasn't working out quite the way I had hoped, in fact things weren't only failing to get better, they were about to get worse – much, much, worse.

CHAPTER 11

Colour Blind (Red Flags)

THE next few years offered enough red flags that even the most obstinate of people would have stopped to re-evaluate their life – not me. I not only ignored them, but went barrelling right on through caution signs like one would if driving towards a cliff. I really didn't see a way out and for many years to come was on the verge of experiencing a state of hopelessness I could never have imagined.

The summer following my final year of university, one bright summer morning after an evening out the night before, I was involved in a tragic motorcycle accident. A passenger on my bike was killed, while I severely damaged a leg and spent months in hospital facing numerous surgeries. Also, I faced a charge as a result of the accident and though the courts didn't consider alcohol to be a factor, I wasn't so sure. I knew it affected everything else I did at the time.

If ever there was a time for a wakeup call, this should have been it. Guilt, shame, remorse, I could have used help with any or all of those. Instead of seeking counselling or therapy, alcohol served the purpose and numbed away all the discomfort – of which there was plenty. The more it worked, the more I turned to it, and the more I turned to it, the more I needed it, the more I needed it, the less control I had. Then finally, without knowing and most certainly without my permission, I was rendered powerless. In a world with far too many addicts as it is, one more was born.

In the meantime, all around me, life went marching on. Friends were getting jobs and establishing careers, some started their own businesses, often trying and failing only to learn they had to try harder. Most were getting married and starting to have families.

I on the other hand felt like I was surrounded by quicksand. I also began to drink alone far more frequently than in the past, as most of those buddies now had responsibilities and lacked the time to do so – that was disillusioning. While they had aspirations and dreams to follow, I kept setting my sights lower, and then finding it increasingly difficult to maintain those low standards. However, I had learned to put up a good appearance, which was important. My outsides never quite matched my insides and while rotting at the core, for all intents and purposes it looked like I was doing okay.

I had taken on work for minimum wage as a security guard at the company across the street from my house. My mom's house actually, in my mid twenties and little to show for my efforts, any money I made went towards partaking in my favorite pastime. One day I managed to muster up the nerve to ask a woman from that company's Human Resources department if we could have a brief chat. I was trying to find a job that paid beyond what I earned as a guard, hoping she might offer some insight as to how to get hired by their firm. She agreed and we met briefly the following week when she suggested I perhaps try and get a job in Production Control, that being a department often hiring. With an undergraduate degree (as tainted and unworthy as I considered it to be) coupled with a course or two, I would likely stand a good chance of getting hired.

I hadn't the slightest idea what such a job might entail, but that was irrelevant. What I required was some direction in my life and for someone to make a decision. As long as it didn't have to be me, I would gladly oblige.

At twenty-five years old without ever having had the slightest idea of what I was going to do for a living, just like that the fog had lifted – Eureka!!! Not just a practical means to temporarily tie me over until I figured out what I was born to do, this was the real deal and my life path was set. It had never so much as crossed my mind that there might be something disturbing about letting a complete stranger decide the course for my future after a 60 second discussion. My insecurity was such that I honestly thought someone who knew me for all of a minute must have a better idea of what's best for my life than I could possibly have known myself.

I took her advice, finished the two courses that were recommended and within a short time was working for the Materials department of a local company that produced metal door frames. In time I went on to work for several other companies in different industries, but always in a similar role. All the while, my increased dependency on alcohol continued to plague me. Afraid of the drastic consequences that might result, my mantra at the time had become; *I'll put an end to this – tomorrow.*

With my degree of drinking escalating, what amazes me more than anything else was my ability to secure most of those jobs in the first place. Who in the world would even hire me? Walking through the forest that day I became aware of the answer to come, which helped explain the paradox and some of the employment related anguish with which I had been wrestling.

CHAPTER 12

The Great Pretender

"HOW can you tell when an alcoholic's lying? His lips are moving." Albeit rhetorical, it's a question I've heard on many occasions over the past few years. It's also one with which I can strongly identify because during those years of drinking my lips were not only moving; they had been moving a lot. Although an awful lot came out of my mouth, the truth was seldom included in that.

Lying is virtually the only reason I was not only hired for any job I ever had, but my means of holding on to it. Whoever initially interviewed me might months later have been asking "where in the world is the person we interviewed for this job?" What they were getting as compared to who they thought they were hiring was entirely different.

Then again, why wouldn't it be? If there's one area I became proficient, it was my ability to be convincing – more accurately, to be deceiving. As I learned many years later I wasn't alone in that regard, for most alcoholics it amounted to nothing short of a survival skill. Back in those uninterrupted years of employment, it all started with a lie and proceeded from there.

I was brilliant in the initial interview, having a tremendous ability to recall all of the outstanding feats I had been part of and the skills that emerged as a result. I had directed committees created specifically to solve customer service related problems, gaining the support of every level of the organization in the process.

I had become a teacher, a mentor of sorts by taking state of the art processes (lean manufacturing for instance) and pontificating on practical terms to those less inclined to understand. I had demonstrated such ability they would not only buy-in to such change; they would do so with enthusiasm. My intuitive feel for analytical thinking and problem solving abilities were such that in the future, half of the company's problems would be solved before they ever came to fruition.

"When can you start?" If I been at the table listening, I wouldn't have been able to wait to hire myself. There was a slight oversight of course. I generally had absolutely nothing to do with these things, except perhaps be the guy to get coffee while others discussed matters of which I couldn't even comprehend. Being employed by an organization and having a colleague who actually did such things, in my mind was tantamount to staking claim to such an attribute myself – so I did and did so very successfully.

After a period of time I probably started to believe some of these things myself, along with the padded academic accreditations I conjured up when asked for qualifications. The conversations in my head were convincing: *I mean really, if I had actually tried at school or been diligent in my work effort, I could have done those things – probably even better.* I just didn't see the point when someone else would do the work and I could take credit.

About the only person who could see right through me and my behaviour was my father – he knew the routine all too well. For many years now he had been sober, actively involved not only in Alcoholics Anonymous, but energetic and driven to the point of being involved in a variety of things he had never before dared to try.

He was like a new man; I both marvelled at and was very proud of him. I had gone with him to many AA meetings while I was in my late twenties, which a few years later seemed kind of ironic. My dad was exiting the world of addiction at the same time I was entering it. If it were a revolving door we could have been there simultaneously heading in opposite directions. He knew where I was headed and although he asked me to join him as way of supporting him, in reality he was just hoping I might hear something. Or at least a seed might be planted for the future.

There was no point of him trying to tell me what my problem was; it wouldn't do a thing for me unless it was self-diagnosed. My dad remembered what little impact it had all those years' people said what was wrong with him – if anything he drank even more. It wasn't going to be any different preaching to me.

I didn't hear what my dad hoped I might and about the only thing I valued out of attending those meetings was looking around at some of the attractive young women in attendance. *Poor girls,* I thought. *Their fathers must be alcoholics too.* It didn't dawn on me until many years later they weren't there for someone else at all; they had actually just clued in a lot sooner than I did.

That was then however, and I don't lament about the past all that often, it's simply not productive, nor does it solve anything. That's not to say I won't wonder at times how circumstances (like the motorcycle accident) might have turned out had I done things differently. As much as anything, I would wish that my dad and I could both have been in and celebrated recovery, and all that goes with it, at the same time. My father would have loved to have spent time with the grandkids that he never saw, as well as see his own son finally claim victory over his own addiction. He died of a massive heart attack (years of heavy smoking and drinking no doubt took their toll) when I had barely turned thirty and was still years away from being willing to surrender anything. It would have been nice, but most importantly, even if not in unison, we did both find a way to break the bondage that held us hostage – that in itself was a miracle. God's timing may not be what I would always like it to be, but that in no way diminishes the fact that it's still a miracle.

Nancy and I had also been married by that time and although

my father might have seen through me, she was probably shaking her head as much as those employers who months after the fact often wondered who they had hired. She no doubt was asking just who it was she had married. I somehow remain employed through it all; on many occasions even she was curious to see just what excuse I was going to use in order to spend another day at home.

Often leaving the house and headed for work knowing I remained in bed and would once again be calling in sick, she then shuddered to think of what the rest of my day might look like. One thing was for sure, I wasn't really ill. If I was sick I would have been up and had left for work long before her. I just didn't believe in staying home when I really wasn't feeling well, it seemed a complete waste of time at home. I may as well be at work, having better plans for those days I would call to say I couldn't make it.

My thinking was increasingly dominated by the thought of alcohol, the obsession was beginning to impact every decision I made, whether aware of it or not. Similar to many alcoholics, I was of the belief the only thing required was a change in circumstances, which would do the trick and remedy the situation. Given the right conditions, I would surely become the responsible man that I should be. I had tried the geographical cure during university and it hadn't worked so well, but behold, there was a better answer. Having kids had made many a wayward man become a new person. Why shouldn't it do the same for me?

So we tried and eventually did, but what transpired beforehand was a telling sign of just how little value I put on the thoughts or feelings of others. Still living in that town in the Niagara region, my wife had become pregnant. I remember being very excited, actually believing quite strongly in the fact that having a child would magically transform me into the man I wished but somehow couldn't quite become. I looked forward to that day when I could put an end to how I had been living and everything was going to change.

"Your wife is going to have to be admitted sir. A miscarriage at this stage requires medical attention that has to be monitored". The nurse rhymed off the words in the manner a pharmacist might when stating the instructions for taking a prescription. *This just couldn't be happening*, I thought.

She had thought there might be some problems several months into the pregnancy, but I just assumed she was overly worried, probably natural for a first time mother. This confirmed it though and I was distraught. So was she, but that didn't matter – at least not to me. I had more pressing issues, not the least of which was shaking my fist and being mad at God. This was intolerable, I was hurt, I was angry, and I proceeded to do what I did best – I drank (for days).

All the while, my wife was stranded in a hospital ward on the same floor as women having abortions. Not to make judgements on them or their decisions, but if there's one thing that I'd be pretty certain about, it's that a woman who wanted a child and lost it, probably would find it somewhat painful to be around those who were voluntarily terminating their own pregnancy – that's the position she was in. If ever there was a time for me to be a supportive husband that was it. Yet I left her to fend for herself, while I went off and got drunk because I felt sorry for myself. I was a lot of things, but a person of integrity certainly wasn't one of them.

CHAPTER 13

One Flew East and One Flew West –
The Insane Years

A horrible reality of addiction, and had I paid attention at any of those AA meeting my father took me to I would have known, over time the disease progresses and only gets worse. I was unique though and what may have held true for others didn't necessarily apply to me. As the founders of AA so aptly described it, I remained under the delusion that I could one day drink like a normal person. All the while, the gates of insanity were closing in with increasing speed. Moving forward it would affect all of my thoughts and choices and I wouldn't even have to be drinking for it manifest itself. Mine had turned into an alcoholic mind.

The truth behind this fact was clearly demonstrated with some of the changes on the horizon as a result of the fact that my wife had once again become pregnant. This time all would proceed well and as result I would once again let God back into my good books – although I remained the author. So it really didn't make any difference.

One of the very first matters to be addressed would be the need for a new car. With an addition on the way I would need something a little more reliable that the 1992 Chevrolet Chevette I had been driving – it was on its last legs. It still got me from point A to B, but I knew it was ready to go – I had the same feeling I used to have with my dog Taddy Brown.

Tad was the first dog I had ever had. My mom was petrified of dogs, but I somehow managed to convince her it would be good for the family. Her concern for my well-being was probably lessened due to the fact that our neighbours German Sheppard bit me as a seven year old and then required stitches after I bit it back.

Taddy was part Spaniel amongst a variety of other breeds – equestrian horse and shortstop amongst them. I've still never seen another that could leap clear over six foot fence to retrieve a ball and in all my years of playing lacrosse and sending balls his way he was flawless from letting anything get past. He even entertained the little kids by climbing the slide at the neighbourhood park. Taddy would literally stand in line and upon his turn, climb the rungs without assistance and always wait a second or two at the top before descending – he knew they were watching and kids came from all over just to see him.

I still feel a sense of joy reminiscing about that dog, being as young as I was, it was a time in my life when things were simple and I had a lot of fun. Age finally caught up with Tad and he was in his nineteenth year it became pretty clear the end wasn't far off. Going to buy dog food, I would never get more than a can a time. I figured it might be his last and would hate to have wasted money on food I didn't need. Ultimately far more money was spent on gas getting to the store than would have been spent on food (I never did think too clearly). Tad finally gave up the fight in August of 1986 and it was a sad day in not only our home but the entire neigourhood – he was one of a kind.

As for that car of mine, a few years later aspects of it reminded me of my loveable pooch. Not that it possessed the same acrobatic skills, mind you, without necessarily intending, it did have to jump numerous curbs, snow banks and negotiate its way through plenty of ditches – it was equal to the task. Similar to the logic I used with Taddy knowing the end was near, I wouldn't put more than a couple of dollars of gas in the tank at one time – it was always its last ride.

Again, that went on forever, and I spent an inordinate amount of time walking to gas stations for containers because I had run out. Not that it was planned that way, but it was a good exercise program at the time. Actually anything good for me would almost had to have been unintended. I couldn't construct a healthy idea if my life depended on it – a day that wasn't far off.

Finally, the car had seen its last ride and the time had come for a new vehicle. Given the fact that an addition to the family was on the way, it would have to be one with a little more room as well. One overcast Saturday afternoon in late spring, Nancy had offered to join me but I assured her it was okay, I would take care of it and promised to bring home something she would be happy with. There was an area of town that had several used car dealerships within close vicinity, so it seemed like my best bet and I headed there knowing precisely what I was looking for.

That spark and desire that most people had when they were committed to doing something right; a job around the house, a task at work or a gift for a wife or a child. That spark was rare in me, but when my alcoholic mind got working it was in full force and I came to life – it was operating at full capacity that day.

That day I was certain of one thing and one thing only. I was coming home with a Station Wagon with reversed folding back seats facing the rear window. My uncle once had one and since first laying eyes on it, I recognized the value of having rearward looking seats. I really didn't care if it cost $1,000 more than it was worth and neither would I have cared if it was bright pink. All I knew is that when I drove that car my kids would be looking out the back window. Of all the criteria that go through one's mind when shopping for a car, that's the only thing that concerned me. I spent $10,000 that afternoon on a car that was purchased for the simple reason fact that my kids wouldn't be able to see me drink while I drove – I didn't even have any kids!!

That would change though – not the insane behaviour, rather

the absence of kids. A few months later my son Tim was born. I was thrilled to be having a child and grasped onto the hope and belief that it would change me as a person – that lingering generational curse might finally be lifted. Of course, I didn't plan on actually doing anything to bring about such a change; I just wanted to will it into existence. Years later I understood the profound truth of the simple statement I often heard in the early days of sobriety: 'if nothing changes – then nothing changes'.

Although it may not have been the catalyst for instilling a degree of responsibility in me as I had hoped, I did however enjoy being a father and having a son to call my own. Among other things, the house became an awful lot busier, and my wife had too much going on to spend time trying to observe what her husband might be up to. I had to laugh at some of the new dynamics around the house, particularly the interaction with a new baby and the animals that had been part of the family well before any kids came along.

We had moved from the Niagara region at that point and lived in a country setting closer to Guelph where we would eventually settle. There was a small lake across the street at the front of the house, with conservation land bordering at the back of our large yard. Work shortages had led to layoffs at my previous job, so I was collecting employment insurance at the time and 'taking it easy'. It was what I perceived to be a well deserved break, feeling no great rush to get back to work. I thought it more important to spend some time with my young son; although I didn't quite put the same importance into exhibiting responsibility as a parent. The rural setting, simply because there was far less opportunity to be caught, was also far more conducive to my customary practice of illegally enjoying beverages while I drove. That reason itself would have been all the incentive I needed to move away from the city. The station wagon served the purpose for which it was purchased extremely well.

CHAPTER 14

Much more than a Dog

A home in the country, along with the wooded surroundings, brought with it an abundance of wildlife. On occasion, one or two of the creatures would sneak in, usually through a sliding door that led to a dog's door in the back veranda. One memorable day, with Tim being less than a year old and at the age where he was able to sit up and crawl, he was enjoying 'Barney' (or something from that era), while sitting on the living room floor watching TV. I was having little success in trying to capture a chipmunk that had been living rent-free in the house for the past few days, but the cats were well aware of its presence. On occasion it surfaced and made for some memorable incidents. This happened to be one of those occasions.

As Tim sat engaged watching TV, across his lap ran our newest visitor, which delighted him. He felt no reason to believe it wasn't simply part of the family. In hot pursuit came both cats, Billy, followed immediately by K.B. The two went straight over his lap, chasing the chipmunk across the room, along a railing and down the basement stairs. Upon reaching the bottom; the chipmunk simply did a U Turn and reversed the process, with the cats once again right on its tail. With slightly less agility and an inability to think quite as quickly as the animals she pursued, in the opposite direction would come our dog Buster who would run right past until clumsily running into a wall. Right beside Tim they all ran once again, as he simply spent the entire time pivoting to watch the real life adventure unfold before his eyes.

A chipmunk being chased by two cats followed by a dog that was always far enough behind to be going the opposite way – TV couldn't possibly compete with the drama that unfolded before him. He laughed hysterically as this went on for the better part of half an hour. I couldn't catch the chipmunk for a few days, but once I did, Tim was sad to see it go. Given my antics and the resulting tension around the house, the animals were a tremendous diversion at the time. They helped ease what would otherwise have been an uncomfortable place to be. None more so than Buster, who arrived a couple of years before Tim.

Several years before she came storming in our lives; the two cats had been permanent fixtures in the house. Not that I was big on cats, in fact when I was kid my dad had run over our own cat in the driveway coming home from work one day and I never even found that particularly disturbing. However, Nancy liked cats and given my lifestyle and the grief it caused, I knew that on some things I had to do whatever could be done to appease her. Before having Tim, we were still living in the Niagara region and I was working at the factory where the scheme was born to create more vacation time. We had decided at the time to get a dog as well. Again, it was my wife's preference and once more it wasn't worth arguing about and besides, I loved dogs and hadn't had one since Taddy.

It had been a pressing issue ever since a young woman in the surrounding neighbourhood had brought several puppies into the medical center where Nancy worked. It seemed like as good a time as any and I agreed that sure, we would go that weekend to pick out a pup from the litter. A few days later, hovering over six irresistible puppies looking back at us, we settled on Buster (as she would later be named), an eight week old Boxer who seemed to possess a certain charm that made her stand out amongst the others. Within four days this young pup was causing nothing but misery and our decision was being seriously questioned.

As I arrived home from work the first couple of days, much to my surprise, Buster would be waiting outside the door to greet me. After getting home from work herself, I would ask my wife why she had left the dog out in the morning. Claiming ignorance, she just gave me one of those looks like I didn't quite know what I was talking about (which more often than not were warranted). The next day, having to leave early for work herself to attend a meeting, she was to arrive home first and once again, after waiting patiently all day, there was Buster to greet her upon arrival – we were thoroughly confused. After mentioning it to a few people who lived nearby, our bubbly and exceptionally cute neighbour Christine, who always had a smile on her face and something positive to say, solved the mystery. While doing some gardening, she was amazed to watch our young pup jump from an upstairs bedroom window to the ground below. Christine was quite impressed, far more so than we were, as a broken screen simply added to the damage our lovely new pet had already caused.

It was a spare room upstairs in which the window had been left open to help let some air circulate during those summer months. Upset to be left alone during the day, Buster seized the opportunity by charging and leaping through the screen to escape, with the fifteen-foot drop doing little to faze her. Seldom did anyone (other than a dog who wasn't nearly as dumb as people seemed to think) have reason to go into that room, so it wasn't noticed for those few days as the process would be repeated. As a result of her antics and penchant for destruction, the aspiring boxer was nameless no more – Buster seemed the perfect moniker. At least the puzzle was solved and taking that option away from her, Buster was now banished to a small room during the day while we were at work. None too pleased; she destroyed absolutely everything while in the home alone. Garbage cans, cleaning bottles, carpets – if it was there; she chewed it to pieces.

Buster was bad enough during the day, but for her own good

she would to have to learn to stay quietly on her own at night, or her days would be numbered. For the first few nights it hadn't worked, as she cried endlessly until allowed into the room. She was given one final chance to redeem herself – the crying only got worse. Nancy couldn't take it anymore and even though there would be a fee to do so, less than a week into this experiment, she felt compelled to take Buster back to the pound on the way to work that next morning. Although it saddened me (there was something about her defiant nature that I loved), my wife was going out of her mind so I said okay and said goodbye to the mischievous boxer I would never get to know.

The following day, I got a call at work from my wife who was distressed at having given up her dog and wanted another, one more suitable this time. So, with my blessing, she would go back to the pound on the way home and pick one out, perhaps a little more carefully I suggested. Walking along the aisles at the pound that afternoon and trying not to think of what would happen to those that wouldn't find homes, she probably would have been willing to take any one of them as they looked with desperate eyes while she paused by their cage. After half an hour, she finally said to the attendant "I'll take that one". And upon handing over a cheque for $100, she left with her dog and as they arrived home an hour later, I was greeted enthusiastically by our new pup as Buster came charging through the door.

Years later, Buster would be there to greet Tim when he came through the door the first time as well. She was very protective, so much so that for the first few weeks of his life while he stayed in a bassinette by our bed, Fort Knox wouldn't have had the protection that room did. The two cats clearly knew something was different and inquisitive by nature, simply wanted to see what all the commotion was about, especially the unfamiliar sound coming from the room. They would try repeatedly to quietly sneak in and get a glimpse, but Buster would pounce from the bed if one so much as stuck their head in the door. For a dog who had a propensity to do anything but stay in one spot by causing havoc wherever possible, much to our disbelief she stayed on that bed for weeks protecting him like he was her own – which she probably assumed he was.

That's about as aggressive as Buster ever got, which is pretty good for a Pit Bull. In-between her time as a pup to when Tim arrived, Buster's identity had been altered. She changed breeds over the course of a weekend she spent at a kennel as a two year old. While dropping her off, we were told by the owner that he would be happy to watch our 'Pit Bull for a few days. "On no, you're mistaken" we immediately informed him, advising of her proper breed and the fact she was a Boxer. 'Okay' he said, laughing, "I'll see you in a couple of days." Sure enough, not longer afterwards, the original owners from whom we got her as a pup confirmed the true breed after being questioned – they were just too scared to tell anyone. Given their reputation, Buster would have been considered a disgrace to her breed. Tallying all the fights she had ever been in, she had an unimpressive record that amounted to something like 1-21. She got beat up by every dog that ever wanted to fight, usually being on her back hoping to play before even realizing she was in a fight. She carried as deep scar on her chest after doing the same thing after encountering a raccoon one day. Buster was known to lose fights to cats, skunks and once had a pigeon send her running with her tail between her legs. Her only victory – she once managed to rip the ear off of one of the kid's stuffed animals, which she displayed proudly for months afterwards.

Aside from her surprising inability to fight, considering she was amongst a breed renowned for their willingness to do so, she also managed to lack some of the characteristics inherent in any dog. I had never met a dog that couldn't swim – in fact I didn't think it was possible. That all changed the day I saw Buster slowly sinking after noticing a toy floating in the water, one she thought would be better suited to be on dry ground as she struggled to retrieve it. One of the two stayed afloat and it wasn't Buster, as I quickly jumped in to rescue her from drowning in a neighbour's pond at that country home. For all that she lacked, Buster more than made up for as being a stable anchor in a home that would soon become even more chaotic.

There would be two more kids to come along after Tim and between the three of them while growing up they would try and do everything imaginable to that dog. From yanking on her tail and ears, to trying to ride her like a horse, almost daily she would be subjected to whatever a toddler would try on a willing recipient. In all those years, not once did Buster so much as even growl at one of them. She just wanted to be loved and part of a family, which she was, all the time loyal beyond what would be expected, as it seems only a dog can be. Buster was the most sensitive dog I had ever known and if hiding while shaking during a thunderstorm wasn't bad enough, she would cry and hide under the kid's beds when there was yelling in the house – which seemed to happen a lot. Most of the storms causing damage to Buster were of that variety, as opposed to what Mother Nature had to offer. It's amazing the type of unconditional love a dog will display and Buster exemplified this, all the while putting up with more than she deserved. Even a dog is affected in an alcoholic home, but she had a role to play and I can't imagine what it would have been like without her. I don't know if God sends dogs to purpose into specific situations – if so, this was one of them.

Many years later, a few years sober and although the family unit had now been broken, we were able to gather as a united front one final time. Buster was to go for her last car ride while we all gathered to say farewell. With the needle gently pushed under her skin, those tired eyes revealed a wonderful sense of joy and peace. Her eyes slowly closed, it all ending with Buster's final sight being that of looking into the tearful faces of each and every member of the only family she had ever known.

CHAPTER 15

Grace Unnoticed

Having always been blessed in many ways, I was never been quite capable of seeing my life that way. Nor could I shake that lack of responsibility my mom had lamented about years earlier. Having a son didn't change that fact and neither did the birth of my two daughters who weren't too far behind him in joining the family.

Amber was born two years after Tim, and couldn't have been more opposite as a baby. While Nancy was pregnant the first time, I remember us being told by other parents some of their nightmarish stories and what we should soon expect. A year later we still had no idea what all the fuss was about. Amber would more than make up for any difficulty her brother managed to avoid and we finally understood what they had been talking about (and took back all these snide remarks that were likely made in the process).

Never one to understand the need for sleep and since she was awake anyhow, Amber saw little reason why the rest of the house shouldn't be awake to keep her company. As might be expected, the only time she did sleep was precisely when we didn't want her to. Her restlessness and constant tugging at the bars to her crib directly resulted in its demise; a custom made crib that had been in the family for three generations and one that was deemed to be invincible – until she got a hold of it.

From the second she could crawl, she was on tables and counters and into everything her overactive fingers could get a hold of. I even had to call poison control once with what no doubt sounded like a fairly odd question – what's the effect of a child having a frog in their mouth? At least it wasn't a live frog, but after spotting something shiny in her mouth, in an effort to remove it before she tried to scurry away, I anticipated finding a wrapper of some sort. She would get into such things on an hourly basis, so it wouldn't have been unusual. As I felt the texture I knew it wasn't what I was expecting and slowly, not to mention surprisingly, appeared a frog – minus one leg (young Amber had a longing for delicacies at early age). Where in the world she found it I had no idea, but considering who was involved, I wasn't the least bit surprised either.

Her carefree nature and propensity for mischief wasn't well suited to the carelessness and irresponsibility displayed by her father – there were bound to be consequences. Some were a little more noticeable than others, such as her run in with a monkey as a three year old.

"What happened to Amber's hair?" I could hear the frantic screaming almost before getting the chance to say hello while picking up the phone at work. Nancy was on the other end of the line getting the kids set for school and daycare, and in so doing Amber appeared sporting a radically different hairstyle than last time she had seen her – there was substantially less of it. Listening to her voice, I was suddenly overcome by that all too familiar feeling of knowing something had happened the night before, not quite piecing together exactly what it might have been.

As the fog began to lift, I remembered taking the two of them out to a pub with a gang from the office on one of our social evenings. We would often get together and have an evening of food and drinks, while playing pool or darts. In the warmer months, we would spend a few hours at the pub after a ball game. Either way, if my wife was working for the evening, I would often pick up my kids and include them in the fun. Without exception, I set out with the full intention of having no more than a drink or two ensuring I didn't carried away, but it never worked out as planned.

Not looking forward to the rest of the phone call, I was thinking of the night before when we had been at a roadhouse in Milton. It's a town west of Toronto and where the company I worked was located. Nancy knew I had gone back to get the kids and asking them that morning about what they done the previous night, Tim's response to the question of who had cut his sister's hair, was that "the monkey did it". While I was on the phone, one of my co-workers popped by to see how I was feeling and when I mentioned this mystery about my daughter's hair and particularly their insistence upon a monkey removing the long dark strands that had taken months to grow, she simply said "Oh my God, you didn't let them do that did you".

One of the accessories at the bar included an old style barber's chair in the front lobby, a chair that has a monkey with a pair of scissors firmly attached to the head cushion. What else would a three and five year old do if left unattended than utilize the resources at hand? As a result, my daughter exhibited a hairstyle quite unlike any girl her age had likely ever seen, compliments of an elder brother who as a five year old would have administered his first and likely his last ever hair cut. All the while, I was in a room far removed from their presence and went about my evening, glancing out the window on occasion to ensure they hadn't left the premises.

Like other occasions, the morning after, my wife quite often had to deal with whatever mess I had created the evening before. I could never understand it, had no concept as to whatever danger my kids might be in and simply thought I should be commended for including them in my activities. As she became more frustrated over time, I again would justify my behaviour to try and put myself in a better light.

She could have had it a lot worse, I would often tell myself. Some guys were off getting drunk and waking up in the beds of complete strangers, or jacking up their credit at strip joints with their buddies – I was simply including my kids in some harmless fun. She should be grateful.

In time Amber's hair grew back, it took a lot longer for my wife to forgive me for my carelessness and even longer for me to shed my irresponsible behaviour. Episodes of that nature occurred on a weekly basis, sometime while with the kids, other times without. What would solve the problem, no one quite knew, but it became pretty clear that having kids wasn't going to solve anything. If two children weren't enough, a third certainly was going to be the answer.

Four years after Amber, along came Shae Lynn, which in itself left me somewhat shocked. Another baby at that point was pretty much the last thing I would have expected, particularly in light of the absence of any amorous activity at that stage of our marriage – generally a prerequisite for such an occurrence. Nonetheless, there I was, a man who had long lost the ability to take care of myself let alone my kids, and I was now a father of three.

As opposed to his first two, who, regardless of the condition I was in, because my wife had worked and spent so much time at school, I spent an inordinate amount of time with and had created a strong bond. This time it would be different. We had moved from that country setting to a new subdivision in Guelph, one where neighbours were constantly around and Nancy was home more having finished her degree. I was long past the point of feeling like being around the house and bonding with another child and deep down (and it wasn't until years later I realized this), I had resented her arrival.

With three kids, there would no way I was ever going get out of a marriage that wasn't working and it would be my baby's fault – someone had to take the blamed and I took it out on her. Reflecting back on it years later, it's pretty sad, but given the self-centered glasses through which I saw the world, it was congruent with just about everything else I thought and did.

After my journey in recovery began, Shae Lynn and I developed a bond that I could barely believe I had almost allowed myself to miss out on. At age 11 in grade 6, she wrote an end of the year paper on a personal hero – and proudly brought it home to show me the A that she received on writing a paper about me. Like so many other times since, I was reminded that Grace is an unmerited gift, as I certainly did nothing to deserve the relationship I now had with the daughter I once used as a scapegoat for my continued reprehensible behaviour.

When people leave recovery too early because things don't work out immediately (and years of instant gratification can make practicing patience a challenge), this is a prime example of the type of reason why I'll simply encourage them to hang on until the miracle happens. I've heard the saying before and couldn't agree more that 'God will always meet us where we're at but never leave us there'. When I finally surrendered a lifestyle gone haywire, God did anything but leave me where I was.

Shae Lynn's is a personality that is quite unique and as she began to approach the age for elementary school, she developed a very strong self-confidence, something she must have got from her mom – it sure wasn't a trait I had ever carried. She simply could not fathom how something couldn't be accomplished with the application of sheer effort. If she wanted something, she saw no good reason why it wouldn't happen and for the most part that was pretty healthy attitude to have.

With all that I lacked in parental ability, it didn't change the fact that I had wanted to spend time with my kids and offer them all they deserved. It's not that I didn't want to be responsible; I just seemed incapable regardless of how hard I tried, or at least thought I tried. Ultimately, my need to drink would always win out in the constant battle between parenting and fighting my addiction.

"Can we have McDonalds for lunch?' Not an uncommon request to be heard by a parent, usually more frequently than preferred. More often than not, for good reason the answer would simply be "no". Such were the wishes of Shae Lynn, who at the time was barely old enough to speak. She was too young to realize that the chances of doing so after church that Sunday morning would be next to nothing. Her brother or sister would have been able to tell her that, good reason or otherwise, they knew the answer would always be 'no'.

We were leaving the Cathedral downtown, a large Catholic church that I would try and get the kids to as often as possible on Sunday's. Given what the rest of the day would look like it was probably pointless, but I thought constituted good parenting – others at church agreed. And I required affirmation of some sort, likely for the simple reason that it mitigated some of the guilt and shame I carried. Without fail, as soon as church ended we would be out the door and off to lunch – the remainder of the day driven by my agenda. There wasn't a chance that lunch would ever be at 'McDonalds', or any facility that wasn't a licensed one.

Considering their ages, those three kids spent an inordinate amount of time around pubs, usually of course while Nancy was at work, which included a lot of weekends. All the same, I was still spending time with them, and in my mind that's what mattered most – in fact it's all that mattered. My distorted thinking couldn't comprehend the danger I was putting them in, or the strain it would put on our family. It was continuing to take a toll on our marriage.

CHAPTER 16

Somebody Likes Me

"So, would you like to get together?" Wow, I thought, it had been quite some time since anyone had asked me a question along those lines, although it did take a second or two to understand the nature of the request. Just about any outing of mine had some adventure attached to it because I hadn't the slightest idea how any one of them might end. Such was the case considering my alcohol allergy and proneness for breaking out in spots.

Gradually, my behaviour was driving me further away from my family, resulting in increasing periods of isolation. The need for alcohol escalated and I was doing whatever necessary to find a few minutes to get some kind of beverage into my system. I didn't appreciate the looks I got from my wife around the house, so I would generally try to limit my drinking at home until everyone had gone to bed. However, there was an entire evening to get through before that happened, so I created a multitude of excuses to get out of the house. Nobody really argued with me, not only would there be little point, it probably offered them a bit of break anyhow.

I would go to pubs on occasion, but for the most part I considered it to be too expensive – I was a cost conscious alcoholic. Instead, I would tour the countryside I had had come to know so well. I knew back roads you wouldn't even find on a map, most of which had cans and bottles in their ditches courtesy of whatever I had purchased at the liquor store for my excursions. One of my favorite excuses was to take Buster out for a good run; she had been home on her own most of the day and this way I also felt like I was doing something useful – nobody was fooled and they knew what I was up to.

There was a long stretch along the river that flowed through downtown and I would usually take her there, conveniently enough it was located a block from a beer store. Off the two of us went, both as happy as could be; she with open space to run around and jump in a river too shallow to drown, me with a couple of large cans of beer at my side. I would often see cars parked along a strip in a certain section of the park, usually mid aged men, quite often reading a book or the daily news. It was a picturesque setting, so I merely assumed these were businessmen taking a break from their hectic schedule.

One afternoon, a day not really much different than most others excluding the fact that Buster wasn't with me, I was passing through the area of town and decided to stop and relax with a few drinks before heading home. Finishing one of the two large cans, I started on the second and decided to keep it well concealed and finish it during the ride home. Pulling out of the parking lot, I noticed (out of a well founded paranoia of police cruisers, nobody checked their rear view mirror to the extent I did) a mid-sized sedan follow immediately afterward. Probably no big deal I thought, I was soon to be turning anyway. I would pass by the elementary school that my kids attended and then meander home through the side streets from there. Right behind me, the sedan followed with every turn and I began to feel a sense of panic. I knew what the outcome would be if it were an undercover police officer.

Please God; don't let it be the police. Just get me out of this and I won't do it again. I didn't have much variety in terms of a prayer life, but I was pretty religious in the frequency with which I used that one.

As the car continued to follow, my primary concern at that point was to ditch the beer and I quickly headed for a nearby gas station. Wrapping everything up in a newspaper preparing to dispose of the evidence, a marked police cruiser pulled into the gas station within seconds of my arrival. While putting $10 of gas in my tank and at the same time hurriedly disposing of my garbage, I fully expected the officer to confront me and check the bin. He didn't, still sitting in his car on the radio, he was seemingly occupied with another matter altogether.

What a relief that was, but the sedan had pulled in as well, with a robust, well dressed man with dark glasses using another gas pump at the same time. Lining up to pay, the same gentleman was in line right behind me and I nervously waited for what might happen next when those words came out of his mouth – "So, would you like to get together?"

It took me a minute to fully comprehend what was being asked, at which point all that could come to mind in the form of a reply was "thanks for the offer, but I'm sorry, I'm not that type." Just as quickly, I had forgotten my answered prayer and the deal I made only moments earlier – God was getting used to it.

As I told the story at work (except I included Buster as being the reason for the visit and neglected to mention that alcohol was involved), I was surprised to learn that exact park that I had frequented all those years was notorious as the prime spot for gays in Guelph to meet and solicit sex.

"How could you not know that" a friend exclaimed. "It's only in the paper every other week". I wasn't much for getting the paper or reading the news, what happened out of my world didn't really concern me (ironically my day of notoriety was coming and I would be the news). It did however make sense, as I thought about the fact that there was always a flow of traffic with men alone in a car, their windows opening and shutting for brief discussions.

What I found especially humorous was that several colleagues (guys basically trying to put up a tough front) were outraged, wondering about my reaction and whether or not I felt like punching the guy, which undoubtedly would have been their immediate response. Quite the contrary I thought, without voicing my opinion. I actually felt quite flattered at the time – I was just happy somebody wanted me.

CHAPTER 17

Powerless – Approaching the End

I couldn't tell you how many times I've witnessed the life altering significance behind an individual accepting the profound truth of what being 'powerless' actually implies. Unexpectedly, for me it also had the greatest impact on the development of my faith. It's like having a front row seat to divine handiwork when watching what happens to someone who has reached the point where they have nowhere left to turn but to God. As I once heard someone phrase it, 'there's something sacred about reaching a bottom'. And as long as they're still breathing, I wouldn't put it past anyone to become a changed person.

On the flip side of course, one's denial and their futile attempt to continue with something they've long lost any control over can be the source of immeasurable misery – I've seen my share of that as well. I need not look any further than my own experience, I had lived it. Although I hadn't quite found my own bottom yet, I was getting perilously close to running out of time.

Included in that swelling obsession that I just couldn't seem to shake, was an ever-increasing need to drink immediately after surviving another workday. As a manner of being able to function when getting home, I made it a habit to stop at the liquor store immediately after leaving work. There was some embarrassment around showing up on a daily basis, so I did my best to stop at different liquor stores and certainly knew enough to approach different tellers – I didn't want to appear conspicuous. I had the routine down quite well. A couple of litre cans of beer and a couple of large bottle of Mike's Lemonade – then a leisurely drive home through the side roads. It would prepare me for whatever situation was waiting.

I sensed it was becoming a problem, in fact many times vowed that I wouldn't do so that evening, but inevitably my car directed itself into the parking lot at 4:40 each afternoon. I tried leaving my bank card at home, tried leaving my wallet at home – I would just borrow money from someone towards the end of the day as the overwhelming urge began to build.

"Hey, whose bike is that?" From my desk that morning, I could hear the question asked repeatedly, each time someone new walked past the lobby, entering to start their work day. Well, I knew the answer, and certainly knew the reason, although I wasn't about to share it with those who had asked. And they did ask, because as soon as the question was answered and they were told "that's Dan's bike", the common response was "is he crazy". For good reason as well, I wasn't exactly accustomed to riding a bike to work, nor did I live around the corner.

This was the summer of the 2002, the year in which it was finally going to come to end and I was desperately trying to hang on to that lifestyle I was so accustomed to. As I woke up that Tuesday morning in July the thought crossed my mind, *maybe I should ride my bike to work. I can't stop at the liquor store on the way home if I do.*

As simple as that I had found the solution to my problem. Forget the fact that I lived twenty-five miles from work and hadn't ridden a bike seriously since being a teen; if I could avoid drinking immediately after work, then I couldn't possibly be an alcoholic. So that's what I set out to prove and if enduring a gruelling two-hour bike ride back and forth each day was what it required, so be it.

I just told the office staff that I was trying to get in shape – they admired my dedication and stamina. I never lost my ability to be the great pretender and one more time, nobody at work at the slightest idea of the battle that had been brewing in my mind.

Our home life had reached the point of being in dire straits and my wife immersed herself in her own activities as I did in mine. For the most part we had become like two ships that passed in the night. However, on occasion those ships would collide, which wasn't pleasant for anyone in the family – actually, it reminded me of the home I had grown up in. Nothing was ever really done to try and address it, of course had we tried I would have merely suggested that if she would change some things, all would be fine. I was pretty quick to blame others and besides, was rather content with the status quo.

By this point my drinking was also being discussed amongst family members, who would try and reason with me but may as well have been talking to a wall – better off actually, at least a wall wouldn't talk back. I was back in that familiar mindset where I simply wished everyone would mind their own business. Besides, my wife and kids, that was really the problem and if not for what they were putting me through, heck, I likely wouldn't drink at all – or at least very little. That theory was soon going to be put to the test, as the rest of the family prepared to fly out west for a vacation to visit relatives. I was staying at home to work, along with tending house and getting some long overdue chores done while they were gone. *Finally, the break I deserve*, I thought, eagerly anticipating their departure.

It was the last Sunday of July in 2002 and I would be dropping them off at the airport early that morning. I did so with great intentions of what I would accomplish the following two weeks in which they would be gone. We made the trip to the airport, I said my good-byes and there I was, a free man, one with something to prove at that. Since I was at the airport on the outskirts of Toronto, I thought perhaps I would start the week with a trip downtown, maybe pop by St Michaels Cathedral for mass. An old cathedral with magnificent ceilings and stained glass windows, it was located in the heart of the city, with several other older churches in the vicinity. I used to love walking through that area when I lived in the city. It was something to marvel and for some reason it had always felt good to be there, as rarely as that was after getting married. So downtown I went; my week was getting off to pretty good start – if only they could see me now. Upon mass ending and leaving church I was feeling upbeat, even invincible – there was nothing wrong with me. I thought that perhaps I should pick it up a notch.

The Pope had been visiting Canada at the time and later that Sunday morning there would be a papal mass outdoors in the north end of the city. After leaving the cathedral, time was a bit of a constraint, but I felt compelled to see him that morning anyway – and I did. Two hours later, there I was, watching with an unobstructed view. The Pope and me, separated only by a three foot wide bar, with a beer in hand as I watched on TV at Hooters restaurant on Adelaide St in downtown Toronto. Keenly aware of the scantily clad waitresses delivering my favorite draft while keeping one eye on the screen, I remember thinking; *you really can't get much more spiritual than this*. I have no idea what the Pope was doing four hours later, but I sure hadn't budged.

And so began two weeks of 'proving myself', barely drawing a sober breath the entire time they were gone. During their absence, aside for that inauspicious first day, there were several notable events that reaffirmed perhaps it was me and not them that was the problem. I had rolled our van in a ditch while on a drinking excursion through the surrounding country roads and a day later while driving a rental vehicle, received a twelve-hour suspension to my license on my way to the liquor store that morning. The police had been notified by a concerned motorist who spotted me dozing off while waiting at a stoplight. Having called in sick to work several times, one day I managed to get kicked off of the same golf course twice for being intoxicated, another, after walking through some trails I managed to lose Buster, only to find her waiting by the car later when I returned after getting sidetracked.

An afternoon phone call from my wife's work woke me, after passing out on the couch that second Saturday after they had left. I realized that in a few hours I would have to leave to meet them at the airport, which sobered me up pretty quickly. All the chores I had planned for those two weeks had to get done in that brief period of time. I had a bit of prioritizing, followed by a whole lot of explaining to do. From that point forward my drinking continued to get worse, which was next to impossible, so it was only a matter of time before something was going to give. I didn't know how to stop, my wife didn't know what to do and the kids didn't know where to hide.

CHAPTER 18

Messages without Words

TIM and Amber both played organized baseball at the time, with the second week of August annually being when the league championship and final tournament was to be held. It was always something to look forward to and after a summer without the games being too serious, the kids got to experience a few days that were a little more competitive than what they had been accustomed. From Thursday onwards, it was one of running back and forth to games, with the excitement building each day as the team advanced further along avoiding elimination. I intentionally had tried to avoid taking anything along to drink, thinking that the least I could do was be a responsible parent for a couple of hours – after all this was important to them. The urge would always become too strong though and I was defenseless towards getting started, always wanting just one drink – nothing more. Under the cloak of generosity by picking up snacks or coffee for some of the other parents, I always found a way to leave and make some much-needed pit stops and satisfy my obsession.

That year Amber's team had made it to the finals, which would be on the Sunday morning. Everyone was excited and waiting in the van ready to leave at 9:00am, as I quickly ran back in to get a glove or something I intentionally forgot in the house. Detouring through the garage (where I kept my supply well hidden) I had several gulps of wine, taking enough of the edge off to carry on. Once started with that first sip, there was no stopping. While the game went well and my daughter's team won, I just kept right on celebrating throughout the day. A few hours later Nancy had gone to work and so began what seemed like a typical Sunday afternoon, except that this one was going to end a little differently than all the others.

After being in and out of the garage all afternoon trying to hide my drinking from the kids, dinnertime was approaching and I was in no mood to prepare something. I had also run out of liquor, which was far more pressing a concern that what the kids might have for dinner, although they were beginning to ask. "Why don't I just get take out" I suggested.

That's all they really needed to hear to realize what my real intentions were and their response was of little significance. There are two things that would be guaranteed, one was I would probably pay little attention to what they said and even more so, I wouldn't be able to look into their eyes when they did.

Today, I sometimes still find it difficult to look into someone's eyes when talking to them, more often than not without even realizing it (until they point it out), however I've come to understand why – I have spent too many years trying not to. It might have been my kids, my mom, dad or step-father, in-laws; regardless of whom, there were far too many times that the look of disappointment in their eyes would be too much to take. The strongest messages I ever received were with words that were never spoken.

On that night, again I had left without looking, so I couldn't see the sadness in their eyes. Their disappointment wasn't because of something they were about to have or not have for dinner, they were simply old enough to know there was something wrong with their father and it had to be scary. I needed something to drink though and that was more important than anything else at the time.

CHAPTER 19

Roll down your Window

Backing out of the driveway I realized that leaving my three year old at home might not be such a good idea – people just couldn't be trusted these days. I left Tim and Amber at home on their own, while I went back to get Shae Lynn and took her along. Not far from the house there was a pub I went to occasionally, the beer was cheap and the food edible – not that it really made much difference to me. I was getting take-out and could have a few beers while I waited for whatever food it was that I ordered. The bartender didn't think it was a good idea for me to have a second, which although I didn't appreciate, wasn't going to argue about – I didn't want to cause a scene. Besides, I had to run out and get cash from a nearby bank machine anyway, so scrambling to look for Shae-Lynn, I finally found her by a gumball machine talking to a patron who offered an unfriendly look as I carted her off.

Returning to pick up the food, I quickly paid and we left, saying hello to a police officer coming through the doorway as we exited. *Somebody's in trouble*, I thought. Turning the ignition while at the same time hearing a tap on the window to see the same police officer standing beside me, I had a hunch as to who that somebody was.

A year later I actually tried to track down that young woman behind the bar, the one who had the courage to call the police that evening. Young, bright, very pretty, she was a student at the university and likely no longer around. I just wanted to thank her – she likely saved my life. I wouldn't have survived much longer living the way I was.

As the police officer escorted me from the driver's seat, I had a strange sensation, almost a sense of relief. For years I had been successfully been avoiding the police, almost daily being in a position where I could have been arrested. I was actually glad it had ended and for whatever reason thought that maybe; just maybe this would be it.

In the meantime, Shae Lynn got to experience the sight of seeing her father handcuffed and put into a police cruiser as she looked out the back window. For years she was terrified by the sight of flashing emergency lights for any reason – never knowing what bad thing might happen next.

On the way downtown, I started to wonder whether or not I was even legally impaired, perhaps it was all a mistake and they would let me go. I had long lost the ability to be aware of whether or not I was drunk and my mind wasn't going to work right regardless, so to me it really didn't matter. To those uniformed law enforcement folks that brought me in it certainly mattered, with the officer who conducted the breathalyzer informing me that I was almost four times over the legal limit – aside from a cell, I wouldn't be going anywhere for a while.

"Excuse me sir, can I see your driver's license please?" It was three years until I would again hear those words from a police officer outside my window. It didn't sound like she was in the mood for a playful conversation.

The boys were in the back causing a bit of commotion, having just come out of the golf course a few minutes earlier. Tim and his friend Robert were just continuing to carry on after getting in the car and as I turned to ask them to settle down, I noticed the flashing lights. There was an immediate sense of panic – for an instant I had that same feeling as years earlier. It was the first time I had been stopped by the police since that night of my arrest.

The golf course was on the outskirts of the city and we were returning home. "Yes officer, I'll be happy to get that for you. Is there a problem?"

I knew the problem. Having just turned on to the expressway from the side road the golf course was on, I had been leaning back and shifting clubs around while in the middle of the road after leaving the parking lot. There was no traffic (excluding her in the distance) whatsoever on the deserted street and I wasn't too concerned. Evidently, she was.

"Well sir, I wasn't too impressed with your driving" she responded.

"My driving; oh, if you think that was bad, you should have seen me on the golf course" – I waited for a response. Nothing, she didn't even flinch. That pretty well confirmed my earlier suspicion that perhaps she wasn't in the most jovial of moods. I wasn't accustomed to joking with police officers, but would have appreciated a smile at least.

"Don't go anywhere; I'll be back in a minute." I didn't think I looked like a runaway convict or anything, where exactly would I go? So, I waited. And although I had no idea what kind of a charge she might come back with, I knew one thing for sure – it wasn't going to be for drunk driving. That was the first time I can remember in many, many years, that I didn't have anything to be concerned about and it felt fabulous. I wasn't sure what she would ticket me for, perhaps it might be for being a smart-ass – I probably deserved it.

"Please be a little more careful and use your side of the road. Have a good night". Well, she may not have smiled, but at least she had a heart; that was reassuring and I couldn't afford a ticket anyway. It was nice to be stopped by the police and a few moments later able to drive away again.

On the night of my arrest while my daughter watched out the rear window and a crowded bar gawked at the scene in the parking lot, there would be no driving away. It would be a while before that privilege was again in place, but I had bigger problems to deal with.

CHAPTER 20

Hanging on by a Thread

GOING home in the middle of the night after being released from my cell wasn't the most pleasant of walks. I wasn't quite sure how to talk my way out of this one and for the first time I could remember, was actually a little bit scared by how out of control my drinking had become. Where was all of this heading?

Okay, I've learned my lesson, I'll never drink again, I replayed those words in my mind over and over for a couple of days. My fear of how little control I had was well founded, because after two days of fear and trembling I was right back at it. I just had to be a little more creative due to the fact I no longer had a vehicle to drive.

My situation was one that I wouldn't have wished upon anyone. It wasn't so much my family and the look of disgust that bothered me; I was used to that. The biggest challenge was going to be work and after calling in sick the first two days I went in that third morning and had a long talk with our director of personnel. She, and management in general were quite supportive, very sympathetic to the fact that I was using alcohol a little too much in an unhealthy manner to cope with a difficult marriage – it could happen to the best of them. That kind of understanding made me feel much better.

I thought perhaps a stint at the Homewood, a treatment facility in my hometown of Guelph, might be of value to me. A large establishment offering treatment in a variety of areas, it had been an integral part of the community since its inception late in the nineteenth century. Among the areas in which it specialized was addiction, with a world-renowned program that attracted patients beyond even Canada's borders.

I had passed it many times; admiring the spectacular grounds and often wondering just what went on in there. Regardless of what it was, I figured for me, it couldn't be any worse than what went on outside of there and it seemed like it might be a nice place to disappear for a month. That's all I really needed, it would help with some of the shame around the house and at work. With my benefit package, I could take a leave of absence for treatment and it would be entirely paid for by my employer. That being the case, I thought it would be best to opt for the deluxe package, I could be admitted to the in-house program and stay for twenty-eight days.

With my pending trial for the impaired driving charge, there were some legal matters to address as well. I almost fell out of my chair when my lawyer spoke of possible arguments that could be used for my defense with a not-guilty plea. Almost four times over the legal limit when arrested and his only thought was how to get me off.

"You've got to be kidding me" I said, "please, let's just get this over with". If there was one thing worse than the thought of the price I was about to pay, it was that of paying none whatsoever. To do so would amount to erasing the entire experience, as if it never happened. That would leave me right back where I started, which was more frightening than anything. I just didn't trust myself anymore and couldn't wait to get in front of judge for the simple reason that with his influence, he might be able to expedite the Homewood admission process.

It was early September and with the lengthy backlog to their facility; I wasn't scheduled to arrive until mid November. I honestly didn't think I could last that long. Once again, on a daily basis, knowing full well the possible repercussions, I would find a way to get booze. It made no difference that I no longer had a driver's license, I was thirsty and was going to get something to quench it. I could ride from my house to the liquor store in eleven minutes (I had timed it) and even though my wife was checking, still kept a supply well hidden.

As the trial approached, I expected the worst, as my lawyer said that given the circumstances of a child involved and the severity of the alcohol content, a jail term was quite likely. I knew I deserved it. However, like I had my entire life, once again I seemed to avoid the consequences I deserved. A couple of factors affected the judge's decision.

I had been taking the odd university course the last year or two, the one and only healthy aspect of my life during that period. Even then, with a forty minute ride home and needing assistance, I had to sneak out early every week from class to reach the liquor store before it closed. The courses were to help to get accepted for an MBA program at Wilfrid Laurier University, just down the street from Waterloo where I had attended years ago. I had applied mostly for the purpose of trying something new to make me responsible. The geographical cure hadn't worked, having kids hadn't worked, but surely a Masters Program would leave no room for my continued antics.

Again, and this is the story of my life, I was fortunate to have been accepted because in looking at my grades for admission, the criteria included only his last twelve months of full time academic study. The entire transcript from that small school in Peterborough, where I did anything but study and had the grades to prove it, was completely disregarded. Only that last year at Waterloo was to be considered, a year in which even though I got off to an extremely poor start, managed to scrape by with the B average I would ultimately need. The only reason for that was a result trying to prove that drinking wasn't my problem, thus spending those six and half weeks of lent doing work instead of having fun. With a late Easter that year, by coincidence it just happened to be the period of time before the final exams – I salvaged the year because of it. With that average, along with a few decent marks to bump it up with those recent extra courses I was taking and I might get accepted into the MBA program – which I did.

The judge looked favourably upon that and on the fact that I had been pre-registered for the Homewood. Aside from a hefty fine and probation period for one year, he sent me on my way, along with the stipulation I stay far removed from any licensed establishments. I didn't know if I could do that and almost wished I had been sent to jail instead. With my lawyer thanking the judge for his leniency, away I went with the expectation I knew better than ignore a judge's orders. Which I did, but that knowledge meant absolutely nothing. I also knew that somebody telling me what I couldn't do would ultimately have no bearing whatsoever on my actions – it scared me.

My probation officer met with me weekly and was rather stern with her warning about adhering to those judge's orders. To no avail, I just carried on drinking to excess, trying with everything in my power not to do so. I would show up at work with bloodied lips, missing teeth and scars resulting from falls off of my bike, only to make excuses and lie about the nature of my injuries. With only a couple of weeks to go, I didn't know if I would make it. My wife was in contact with Debbie, my probation officer, and at the next meeting she basically gave me an ultimatum. "If you don't smarten up and are found drinking, you'll have been deemed to have broken parole and will be back in front of a judge. Do you understand?"

"Yes" I said, genuinely apologetic, and walked out of that meeting terrified, unable to believe that I could have put myself in such jeopardy. As frightened as I was, five minutes later I was sitting in a bar two blocks away with pitcher of beer in front of me. That fear and resolve had vanished within two blocks – the need to drink was stronger. Knowing I was risking absolutely everything, I sat there shaking my head at my own stupidity. More than that though,

I was just happy to have a drink in my hand. Hours later I staggered into the house after taking the bus home.

"Good morning Dan, this is Rebecca from Homewood's addiction program." I wasn't sure what she wanted, but I had seldom felt as nervous. Surely they wouldn't be calling to cancel at this point would they? Had my probation officer been in touch with them? This was all that was running through my mind as I was caught off guard with that phone call at work that Friday morning.

"We've had a cancellation for Monday and I know its short notice and a couple of weeks earlier than you had planned, but we would like you to come in next week if you can". Maybe God didn't think I had two weeks left in me either, because with that extremely rare last minute cancellation, the impending doom was lifted and I would no longer have to feel like I was hanging by a thread.

"Of course, I replied. Thanks for calling." I decided to spend the last couple of days by taking the kids to my mom's in Oakville that weekend; feeling relieved that come the following Monday I would get a one month reprieve from it all.

My mom had been a Godsend all those years; I'm not quite sure where I would have been without her. It couldn't have been easy having an alcoholic husband and then a son who followed in his footsteps, but she did her best. She had always worked hard and provided for me, helped get me to sporting events and typing my essays when they were two weeks late and to be handed in the next day. After warning me about any of one my many hair brained decisions only to see it blow up in my face, she would always welcome me back with loving arms anyway. She was a fabulous grandmother to my kids and the three of them sensed her home as being a safe haven whenever they visited, a rare time where they could relax and just be the kids that they were.

Several months into doing without a car, we were getting quite used to taking buses, as we did on that weekend visit. I actually behaved myself while we were there, knowing I just couldn't take

DAN MATWEY

the look of sadness that would come over my mom's face knowing I was drinking again. She had been praying about this day for a long time and the devout Catholic that she was, there was probably even a patron Saint specific to that cause (knowing the alcoholics I do and their stories, there may even be an army of them). I remembered as a kid she would pray to St Anthony after losing something almost daily. Him being the patron Saint of lost articles, he was in high demand around our house.

The weekend went well and we said our goodbyes, but on the way home I was beginning to panic knowing what the next morning would bring. I had been told not to use any substances for several days before arriving at the Homewood, but a sense of uneasiness came over me that I could no longer stand.

There were several buses to catch going home and at each terminal I would send the kids off with some change to play a few video games, while I would quickly sneak into a pub for a few quick drinks. After several stops and repeating the process, I felt much more comfortable by the time we had arrived home in Guelph. There was still one final city bus to catch and the terminal was in the roughest part of downtown, the area one would go if they were looking to purchase drugs, or perhaps find a woman inclined to perform favours. At that time of the evening it was dark and wasn't a pleasant place to be for an adult, let alone a child. We had just enough time to catch the 6:15 Route 20, the final one that evening which would stop in our suburban neighbourhood. It was 6:10 and the bus would be arriving any minute.

I told the kids to stay put, asked Tim to keep an eye on his sisters and said I had to run across the street to use a washroom (they knew exactly what I was doing). In the most frightening part of town, I left three terrified kids, a nine, seven and three year old on their own, because at that moment it was more important for me to have a drink than be concerned for their safety.

It was an Irish pub a few doors from the bus stop and I walked in and ordered a pint of beer while standing at the bar. Seeing a digital clock that said 6:13 as I received my drink, I asked for another – there was plenty of time.

Please God, let the bus still be there. There it was again, that familiar prayer of desperation I had said so many times throughout my life – I haven't had to say one since.

I quickly gulped down my beer and ran across to the bus that was still waiting, but getting set to leave. I jumped on as the door began to close; finding three confused kids huddled together quietly by the back window where they had been watching to see if their dad would remember they were there. The only good that comes from that memory is that nearing nine years later; it remains to be their last of seeing their father drink.

CHAPTER 21

Looking for Seagulls

MONDAY morning bright and early, there I was at the doors of the Homewood, set to enter my temporary home for the next month. To my relief, not nearly as scared as I had thought I might be. With a duffle bag I had packed earlier that morning on one arm, and an armful of books on the other, a kind gentleman with a calming voice escorted me to my room. As we walked, he spoke of his role as a volunteer and of the attributes of the facility, which I suspiciously eyed as he carried on with enthusiasm. I wasn't certain what I would be doing for the next twenty-eight days, but was pretty sure I would have a lot of spare time on my hands. There likely wasn't a pub on the premises, so I thought some books might come in handy. To look at me, you would have sworn I was going on vacation – which was exactly what I thought I was doing.

I heard a lot of interesting things those first couple of days, during which I was a willing participant to the extent that I said all the words that seemed to sound right; those old job interview skills were coming in handy. More than anything though, I was a curious observer and spoke as little as possible. People were talking with excitement about change, others were getting emotional as they began to comprehend the devastating impact and pain their actions had caused, and some (many in fact) flat out just wanted to get lost and go drink or smoke something – me, I just wanted to be left alone.

As much as alcohol had reaped havoc all my life, I wasn't really there to learn how to quit drinking – I had tried that and it didn't work. I was never able to make it more than a couple of days into Lent, continuing to try since those university days when I got through the entire forty. So if I couldn't do it, I didn't hold much hope that those kind folks would be able to do much for me. I had made a mess of things and just wanted to get away from the house and to get away from work for a month. Just as important was to stick it out and make a good impression to appease the courts and my probation officer – she was becoming somewhat of a pain.

Essentially, I was there for absolutely all the wrong reasons, but something supernatural was about to happen anyway. I'm no theologian, in fact I'm not even much of a thinker, but as I look back on that period, I've become convinced that God doesn't make it mandatory that one possess all of the correct motives if He is going to have an impact on their life. Given the right circumstances, even with just the slightest crack to gain entry, He can start to work on anyone.

The right circumstances for me were that I wasn't drinking – that's it. Then, and only then, might I be capable of being receptive to anything. It had been a long time since those conditions existed, but there I had no choice and day by day my mind was getting clearer. I was even beginning to show a little more interest in the recovery program what was going on all around me. Not enough to fully engage – but interested nonetheless.

The first significant breakthrough was right around the corner and the effective change it brought about would also solve the first half of the equation for this employment paradox I was trying to answer almost nine years later.

It may not have explained why I would lose jobs in sobriety after I had left the Homewood, but it sure offered some clarity, or at least confirmed what I thought as to why I remained employed during that period beforehand. During those years of drinking, it turns out that lying really had been my most powerful weapon all along. Remove that and I would no longer be capable of fabricating stories like I once had. All that would remain to draw upon would be my own experience – that wouldn't impress anybody. So the natural question was, if lying had been working so well all along, why bother changing at all?

I remember the exact instant it happened. It was like walking towards a doorway wearing chains and walking through the other side having had them removed. And it was an extremely simple practice that comes as second nature to most people.

Should I keep my mouth shut, or shouldn't I? That was the question running through my head for several minutes as the discussion went around a circle moving ever closer to it being my turn to speak. It was Friday and my fifth day of sobriety – a miracle in itself as I hadn't had five total (let alone consecutive) days of sobriety in the past twenty years. I was at my 8am meeting with the core group with whom I would spend my entire program (not unlike what you would have seen in the Sandra Bullock movie '28 days', which I've since felt to be a fairly accurate portrayal of a treatment facility). We were continuing with 'check in' as it was referred to, an activity where each individual in our group took turns stating their name, their drug of choice, their dry date, the way they were feeling, etc. For me, every morning since my arrival on the 4th of November, I would state my name; say that my drug of choice was alcohol and that my dry date was Nov 1st, several days before that last drink at the Irish Pub while I left my kids stranded with them hoping I would return. For whatever reason, on this a particular Friday, instead of doing what simply felt comfortable, I broke a pattern years in the making. I decided instead to do what I knew to be the right thing.

Along with our name, preferred substance (and there's a plethora of choices that will do the job for an addict) and dry date, there was always a question to go along with 'check in'. The counsellor that day had challenged us to share something with the group that we hadn't yet been honest about. I had about thirty seconds to decide and with every ounce of courage I could muster and against every single acquired instinct, I said it. "I lied about my last drink. It was actually Nov 3rd the night before I came in here."

I had originally felt too ashamed or even scared to say I had drank the night before arriving, as during the pre-admission process it's requested of patients to abstain for a period of time (a week was suggested) before starting the program. I thought that by telling the truth they might not let me stay, so all week I had been lying, what else could I do? Now the truth was out and I waited … and continued to wait. Expecting to be told to pack my things, after what seemed like an eternity, one of the counsellors finally said, "It's about time you were honest about something – welcome to recovery."

That was it. To this day it is perhaps the most exhilarating experience of my life, my first moment of honesty in more years then I could remember – life hasn't been the same since. Not on the employment front, that's for sure, as I would soon find out. Adding honesty to the agenda would destroy my mastery over job interviews, one that had been entirely based on lies.

The rest of my stay at that treatment facility went by in what seemed like a flash, much to my amazement, as I absorbed everything they could throw at me. As for those books I had brought, I never so much as opened one. I read through AA's Big Book three times while I was there, simply amazed that twenty five years before my birth a book would be written that would describe my life to a tee.

I was learning about addiction as a being disease and was overwhelmed to understand I had an illness and wasn't the drunken reprobate I had come to think of myself as being. Others who had once been just like me were now free men, and I could be too – I had hope for absolutely the first time I could remember. There are a million books on recovery though, with much better insight than what I could possibly offer in that regard. Suffice to say,

I knew something had happened. Something I was incapable of orchestrating on my own. What I did know and knew with absolute certainty was that somehow God had used that facility for my restoration.

I still spend time there when I can, I love that place. That building I used to drive by and snicker at when I thought of what might go on inside, has quite possibly become my favorite spot on earth. I now know how Eddie Rickenbacker must have felt when he used to walk along the piers of Miami every Friday night with a bucket of shrimp in his hands.

It was a story I first heard the former pastor (Don) of Kortright church in Guelph speak of and one which Max Lucado makes reference to in his book 'Eye of the Storm'.[2] Eddie was fighter pilot in WWI, so proficient in fact he was awarded a Medal of Honor as a result of those efforts. After the war he went on to become very successful in business, including time spent as the CEO of one America's largest airlines at the time. Well respected for service and his skills, he was leading a team on an envoy to deliver a confidential message during WWII, when along with his seven-member crew their plane went down in the Pacific Ocean and they remained adrift on a raft for twenty-four days. Hundreds of miles removed from civilization, after eight days, long after their rations of food and water had run out, they were suffering badly and their prospects bleak. As a last resort they turned to prayer, in desperate need of a miracle – one that arrived later that day in the form of a seagull.

Out of nowhere, hundreds of miles from where one might typically be found, it landed on his head. Feeling its presence, he reached up and without it so much as trying to budge; he was able to grab hold of it. After eating its flesh, they were able to use the carcass to attract fish, then continuing the process, they were rescued weeks later. He never forgot the answer to that prayer and feeding shrimp

---

2 Lucado, Max. *In The Eye of the Storm* (Tennessee, Thomas Nelson Publishing, 1991) Pg 225

to the seagulls all those years later was merely a testament to the gratitude he felt.

Much to the displeasure of many I know who hear such stories and voice contempt at what they deem to be fanciful thinking that God actually could – even would – intercede in life circumstances, I realize I probably once might have once felt the same way. Now I not only acknowledge it with reverence, but because of my own drastic changes that couldn't possibly have been brought on by myself, it's created an insatiable desire to know about this God whom I once felt to be so distant.

This was the beginning of a new life for me, when at age forty-two, was experiencing things for what seemed like the first time. After leaving that treatment facility, I became immersed in recovery and equally so in a pursuit of understanding this God who had rescued me from the abyss – maybe there really was something to this concept of Grace after all. And maybe it wasn't simply about what happened a few thousand years ago – this thought of a God present here and now – it was like I had heard it for the first time. So filled with enthusiasm and driven like never before, I was determined to take that knowledge and find my place in the world – before long including the search for a new job.

CHAPTER 22

New Pair of Glasses

To a casual observer, my way of living wouldn't be considered one worth getting overly excited about – if anything, the exact opposite, after I left that facility. Living on my own in a run-down apartment of a dilapidated building, losing the right to drive a car, having had a marriage that failed, and now a self proclaimed alcoholic – for all intents and purposes a pretty miserable failure by world standards. I had never felt such freedom in my life.

Opting not to return to my comfortable middle class home in the suburbs, I took an apartment downtown in what would have to be considered the roughest area of town – close to where I had left my kids while having that last drink. With the aroma of tobacco (along with other inhaled substances) continually present and the lingering odour of alcohol throughout the building, it wouldn't have been my first choice to live, but was all I could afford.

I had reapplied to the MBA program that had been put on hold for a year the previous September. Although full of anxiety and sometimes questioning just what business I might have being with students far more accomplished than I could dream, it was still something to look forward to. Aside from my stay at the Homewood, I had never finished anything I started. There would be times throughout those three and half years of attending part time that I had wished I began with something a little less formidable, however, I persevered.

I was back at work as well and after having been away for a month to get clean and sober, expectations from the company were high, and rightly so. My employer had paid a sizeable amount of money for treatment and it was time for them to realize a return on that investment. Finally a company might get a reasonable likeness to the guy they thought they would when he used to tell all those impressive stories of great accomplishments in order to get hired. However, it wasn't to be, at least not there. Life might have been getting better, but work certainly wasn't. I clearly remember the day it happened, knowing immediately it would be extremely difficult to maintain that job which I had held for all those drunken years.

"Hi it's your mom; I wish I didn't have to tell you this, but Bruce died this morning. I don't know how to let your brother know either". It would be the first time in many years that I would actually be in a position to be of help, as opposed to a hindrance to my mom. I was quick to reply. "Don't worry about it. I'll make sure he finds out, you just take care of what you have to."

My stepfather had been ill with cancer for five years and the end had been imminent for quite some time. He was a man of tremendous faith who very graciously handled his terminal condition and I was extremely grateful he managed to hang on as long as he did until that spring of 2003. It had allowed him to see another side of me, one that he was probably beginning to think that not only himself, but anyone else would ever live to see. For years Bruce had seen me cause my mom nothing but misery, and certainly experienced his own because of my behaviour. To have been able to talk to him and express heartfelt sorrow for my actions was a blessing. More importantly, it was reassuring that Bruce would leave knowing the wife he left behind had one less thing to worry about – she had enough of that as it was.

I had a brother and sister who were two and three years older than me respectively. During those childhood years, when life sailed along nicely and I was a pretty well adjusted kid, those two were who I most looked up to – not that I would ever have told them that. As time went by and I was in high school and them at university, their lives began to take a turn for the worse and something was clearly wrong.

First with my sister and shortly thereafter my brother – in due course a diagnosis of Schizophrenia had been verified. Throughout the years they had both been an awful lot brighter than me, were very popular, were gifted students and even athletes (in his last year of Junior Hockey at St Mikes my brother was selected as a Western Conference all-star center, with the gentleman selected behind him in that position later going on to gain notoriety wearing number '99'). It has been difficult for them throughout the years, but to this day they both continue to lead productive lives and shown a lot more courage than I ever could have under such circumstances.

At the time of Bruce's death, my brother was in one of the lower times of his life, very much disconnected from society and his family. I had promised my mom that I would track him down, but had very little information to do so – no address or phone number. Essentially, just the neighbourhood in which he lived, from there I would have to figure out the rest. Only a few months removed from having had my license suspended, I took the train to Union Station in Toronto. From there I would proceed to Parkdale, the area of the city in which he lived.

I recall it being extremely warm for mid April, a perfect occasion to make the three-mile trek by foot instead of public transit. With everything I was trying to digest, I loved walking these days anyhow – I just didn't expect this to be one that would have such a lasting impact.

Leaving the downtown core I could feel the familiar breeze from the lake, as the bright morning sun reflected brightly off of the towers comprising the skyline. I was a an hour or so into my stroll when passing what was formerly a well known mental institution in the city, referred to simply by its street number – '999 Queen'.

It had since become a mental health facility, humanized to a large degree as compared to the stigma that once was attached to its common perception as an insane asylum. As a result of its location, this Parkdale neighbourhood to which I was heading was also home to many of the patients of that facility. Far more so than in days gone by, they are now encouraged to integrate with society.

I vividly recalled my high school days, often staying at my grandmother's house that was in the vicinity. It allowed for a quicker trip to school than from my mom's house in the suburbs. Either with my hockey equipment and heading by streetcar to a game, or even just on the way to visit a friend, whenever I came in contact with any of these folks I was scared – hiding in a corner seat just hoping they would soon disappear.

That day I went looking for my brother was different; in fact there was a world of difference. Whereas once upon a time those people frightened me, I actually spent time talking to some as I walked along enjoying the bright sunshine. They weren't frightening, if anything they were scared, or just plain lonely. Why hadn't I ever noticed? Maybe it was spending time in a treatment centre (which also would have been considered a sanatorium only a generation or two earlier) that allowed me to have empathy, but whatever it was; I had meaningful conversations that day.

I will especially remember David, who in a wheelchair was waiting inside the door of a convenience store I had popped by to pick up water. David obviously had some conditions that would have rendered him 'different' at first glance, but as we talked the more intrigued I became. David hat been waiting at the door because there were people in line and out of courtesy he wanted to wait until they were gone, merely wishing to thank the proprietors (an elderly couple that ran the store) for being so kind to him in the two years he had lived there.

That day was his last day in Toronto and he was heading to northern Ontario and going back home. He was taking quite a

DAN MATWEY

risk since he had become so comfortable the past couple of years adjusting to where he was. He just felt that it was time to go. He also spoke of hoping to have a girlfriend one day, having spent time watching couples together and admiring the sense of happiness they seemed to have that others didn't – he would like to experience that himself. I almost cried listening to him, here was guy who by all appearance was a misfit, yet his dreams and aspirations were no different than anyone else – and his mannerism was such that he seemed like a man of great integrity.

These were the people I used to be afraid of? I'll never forget the feeling of shame at that moment. Reflecting on all those years of having simply judged them and written them off as second class citizens – these folks had more character in one finger than I possessed in my entire being. I had a few more conversations that day moving toward my destination and then with a momentary flashback, out of the blue it hit me. Twenty-five years late perhaps, but at that moment I understood.

It was grade 11, during one of Father Hibbard's classes back in high school at St. Mike's. He was one of my all time favorite teachers and would certainly be amongst those I considered to have personally sacrificed a lot to both serve God as priest and teach at that school. He talked openly of the difficulty and frustration that's comes with the territory because of his vocation as a celibate priest. I appreciated his willingness to share so openly.

In class we were discussing a newspaper article that had recently been published in one of Toronto's daily newspapers. The journalist who wrote the story had recently spoken to Pierre Burton upon his return from India when he spent some time in Calcutta. Pierre Burton, who has since passed on, was the quintessential Canadian author and historian, esteemed and well respected across the country.

In this particular interview, in response a question he had been asked, Mr. Burton replied, "If anything ever proved to me that God does not exist, it's what I saw during my time while in Calcutta". Very interesting and fair enough was the tone that came across from the woman writing the article, he probably wasn't the first person to express such sentiments.

What she had also decided to do in order to get another perspective was to see if she could arrange to speak with Mother Teresa, who did her work out of the same location. She had been drawn to Calcutta and established her order "Missionaries of Charity" in that impoverished area of India.

The journalist succeeded and managed to spend time asking some questions and amongst her thoughts came the following reply to question similar to that asked of Pierre Burton. "If anything, ever proved to me that God exits, it's what I see while doing my work in Calcutta."

It did nothing for me at the time, but twenty-five years later walking along a busy sidewalk in downtown Toronto the significance of that reality stopped me in my tracks. How incredible it was that two extremely intelligent people could look at exactly the same thing, yet draw such radically different conclusions. This was exactly what I was feeling while walking along that busy sidewalk in Toronto that day. What I was looking at was absolutely no different than what I had previously looked at, yet what I saw was entirely new.

I was approaching the area of town where my brother lived and looking for the types of places that by describing his appearance, someone may have an idea of his whereabouts. There were a couple of shelters in the area, PARC (Parkdale Activity Recreation Center) and St Francis Table, both of which served into the marginalized members of society. After described him, the feedback I received indicated he did in fact frequent both places and lived nearby, which was good to hear – I was on the right track.

I was directed toward a crowed small cafe, one that appeared to do very little in terms of business, but likely served a great purpose in giving patrons a place to stay warm and dry for a discussion. An elderly gentleman with a warm smile and boisterous personality seemed to know everyone there and knew exactly who I was referring after asking about my brother. He pointed me towards the building in which he lived, where I waited and not long after he came around the corner. Walking right past me as I sat on the stairs reading, he finally noticed me after calling his name several times.

We spent some time together that afternoon, with me wondering why it was I could engage so easily in a discussion with a complete stranger, yet found it tough at times to talk to my own brother. With straggly hair, a beard looking like it had never been trimmed and appearing frightfully skinny, he didn't look good at the time. In fact, he was in about as low a place as he had ever been. That would soon change and he never actually went back to that Parkdale location. After the funeral he settled in Oakville, taking an apartment near my mother's house. With her continuous support, and that of a community agency, over a period of time his health improved and he got back on track, taking on part time work as well. He is in a much better spot in terms of his health today than he was then. An awful lot changed in a few people's lives over the course of a three-mile stretch that day.

CHAPTER 23

You're Fired – Come Back after you've been Drinking

WHAT really stuck out while visiting those two shelters that day was the various staff and volunteers, and observing how they went about their duties. It had a tremendous impact as I watched them try and offer a little bit of dignity to those who were otherwise shunned by most of society. They likely made minimum wage, if anything, while doing so. For the first time in my life, I was convicted with a sense of just how meaningless my own career had become.

My job was never the same after that. It was only a short period that I had been back to work and if before entering recovery, when I was perpetually either hung-over or in a complete fog, my employers might have had 5% of my brain – now they had absolutely none. My mind was forever racing, beginning to question everything, every aspect of life, with my career being the most pressing at that moment.

Why in the world was I spending my time working at a job that did absolutely nothing for me? Eleven years at that firm, and seven more elsewhere working in Production Control all because some woman had suggested it years earlier after a one-minute discussion – that's what I had pinned my future on. Not only didn't I like what I was doing, I never had. It just didn't matter before.

I tried my best to put up a caring front and maintain some

degree of competency at work, but my mind was anywhere but on the job. I would write recovery stories and spend my time staying touch with other addicts. I even had a daily meeting with a machine operator in the plant that had entered sobriety three months to the day before I had. My mind was racing in every which direction but none that was remotely related to the task at hand in my job – and it was becoming blatantly evident. As result, a couple of months later, those words that would eventually become very familiar, were heard for the very first time. Greg rounded the corner and gently tapped me on the shoulder.

"Dan, can you please come and see me in my office." There were two of them waiting, the director of personnel along with him. That chat was more nerve wracking than any interview I had ever had. They went on to express how I had become a disappointment after investing so much time and money in me. I was defenseless – they were absolutely right.

Five minutes later I had walked out the front doors experiencing a job dismissal for the first time in my life. I wasn't quite sure how to feel, let alone what to do.

At least it would give me chance to focus on school, which was certainly a positive to take from suddenly being without work. My MBA program was about to get under way that same week. It had been many years since I had spent time seriously studying and I could use the time. Upon further consideration I realized I had actually never spent time studying – that was frightening. What had I gotten myself into?

CHAPTER 24

A New Chauffeur Please

A night after losing my job I was en route to my very first class of graduate school and was almost overcome by fear – although not to the extent that my friend Rama would experience a couple of months later.

After adjusting surprisingly well at school and even appreciating the free time I was unexpectedly given through the job loss, I was also back in the position of having the right to use a car again. With my licence reinstated and winter approaching, I had offered to drive a classmate to school throughout the winter. She was petrified by the snow and the thought of driving in it. The fact that she hailed from Bangalore (India) and was fairly new to the country, made it understandable that she hadn't had an awful lot of practice driving in icy conditions. Her husband had convinced her to find someone from her class who also lived in Guelph, which is how we initially got connected. "Not to worry", I offered in a reassuring manner after she initially asked. "I've got you covered".

"Please do me a favor and if the machine starts beeping while I'm gone, just blow into it. I'll be back in a minute." It was our first ride together and a feeling of panic came over her as she heard those words while I closed the car door behind me. Rama didn't know whether to get out and run or sit there and cry, but she knew one thing for sure. If she owned a gun and her husband was anywhere nearby at that moment, she probably would have shot him.

Part of the legislation for anyone convicted of an impaired driving offence in Ontario included as a part of the suspension, a portable breathalyzer in the car as being mandatory for a one-year period. The ignition interlock device ensured that the driver had to maintain a zero alcohol content level in order for the car to start. Aside from detection when starting the car, the device would randomly engage while driving and failure to provide a sample, or providing one that detected alcohol would activate an alarm and the engine would shut down within a minute. Providing a proper sample involved a precise method of blowing and then humming until the click sounded, indicating that all was good. It really wasn't as easy as it sounded and during the few months I'd had it, with three kids in the car shouting conflicting advice simultaneously, it became even more difficult and at times downright comical.

"Hum", "Blow", "Hum longer" – "ruff" – even Buster chipped in with all the excitement in the confined space of that hatchback. I messed it up many times over the course of the year, leaving us stranded at the side of the road with an alarm sounding for a few minutes while we all took turns blaming one another. Within a couple of minutes it reset automatically and I would start the process again. Aside from the humiliation, like on occasion stopping at red light beside a car full of teenagers only to sit there blowing into what was obviously a breathalyzer while they glanced, giggled and commented, I was just glad to be able to drive again. The embarrassing moments came with the territory – consequences for my actions (a phrase my kids got extremely tired of hearing years later).

I would even drive around looking for RIDE (police roadside checks) program so I could roll down the window if a test was requested by the officer and respond "no thanks I've got my own". That never materialized, which was probably a good thing, but as far as the police were concerned, I just enjoying the freedom of looking for, instead of trying to avoid them for a change.

Such was the predicament with Rama that evening. She was

stuck in a car with a guy she didn't really know, who as they drove, was blowing into a machine every few minutes for reasons she didn't understand. Then, upon stopping to run into a store as the car was running I asked her to blow into the machine if it beeped – there had to be a good reason for this she thought. "Oh yeah, it's because my husband doesn't trust me to drive, yet will put his trust in this yahoo who clearly has some problems" – actually she wouldn't have needed a gun right about then, she would have killed him anyway.

I went on that evening to explain both the nature of the device (also knowing it wouldn't go off while in the store, having done so less than a minute earlier) and my journey over the past year. Her sense of uneasiness began to subside and over the course of that semester while continuing to drive together, we spent a great deal of time discussing all aspects of life and remain good friends today, long after our schooling.

Virtually every time I gave someone a ride that year, because of that device, I could feel their degree of uneasiness which would instantly take hold. If it were still the day and age when there was an abundance of hitchhikes, I likely would have stopped at each opportunity to pick one up – if for no other reason than to see how long they might last before requesting to be let out. It might have been juvenile, but I enjoyed having that kind of fun – it had been a long time.

DAN MATWEY

CHAPTER 25

Earning Trust Again

For strangers not to trust me was one thing, and looking at a blowing device in a car and drawing the inference as to what it meant – I would have felt the same way. They hadn't known me before, so I may as well have had some fun with it, which I did. Those who were closest to me however, that was an entirely different story. Theirs was a lack of trust based on years of witnessing my behaviour and from being hurt. When or even if it ever came back was beyond my control, however over time I found that it did.

"Dad, can I have 5 dollars? I want to get some french fries", Tim asked. "Just wait here and I'll be back in a few minutes". I'll never forget the day he made that request.

It was Thursday Sept 4, 2004 at Glen Abbey golf course in Oakville for round 1 of the PGA's Canadian Open. We had spent the morning following the likes of Phil Mickelson and Jesper Parnevick (who with his legion of the Swedish Army following along was Tim's favorite). Vijay Singh and recent Masters winner and Canada's newest hero at the time, Mike Weir, were scheduled to tee it up in the afternoon, so we had a full day planned. It was exciting to be able spend the day just hanging out together and talking, as we walked and followed any one of a number of different groups. That tournament was something we hadn't done before, but have since tried to make an annual tradition of attending together.

There was special significance though and it had absolutely

nothing to do with golf. I was aware of it the second he asked, knowing at the moment Tim was feeling something I had always hoped to experience myself as a kid.

Regardless of whether I was at a sporting event with my dad, or out shopping somewhere and planning to meet up a certain amount of time later, it didn't matter. We could be on vacation, or even at the dentist when I would be met in the lobby by the dental assistant and told to wait a little while as my dad was just a having a bit of nap. I never had the security of knowing at any particular time, that when I next saw my dad he wouldn't have been drinking. It was an awful feeling that sat in the pit of my stomach, one that no kid should be subjected to.

As we were at the Open that day, it was approaching two years since my last drink. Tim, as the oldest of my children, would have been most affected by what transpired over those years leading up to that evening in November of 2002 – way too familiar with that feeling in the pit of his stomach. Finally, and long overdue, for the first time in his life Tim knew that he could leave for five minutes knowing when he came back his dad wouldn't have a drink in his hands. This was the day my son started to trust me again – I didn't know if I deserved it, but I sure would take it.

It's also something I heard a lot of during my years a volunteer facilitator for an aftercare program at the Homewood. The group would be comprised of people who had gone through the same program I had, or one similar at another institution. It was nine months in length and that first year, to be around anyone diligently working a recovery program was fascinating to watch and be part of. It was literally like seeing a miracle unfold before my eyes.

In their excitement, there would often be a level of frustration for those who were committed to change, but from others close to them (kids, spouses, and parents) they couldn't regain their trust. That was a delicate area in my own my journey back, and I had to remember those ill feelings were grounded on some pretty solid experience. I had a wonderful sponsor (who my kids named wise Dan) those early years who often reminded me of that. Essentially, I had no control over how other people felt and wouldn't find any peace in trying to do so.

It was a catalyst to some of the most significant freedom and growth I experienced in recovery, as ultimately I could either beat my head against a wall or learn how to trust God with it – that took a lot of work. That's about the most important thing I could share with those men and women in that aftercare group I helped with. Two things helped me more than anything in that process, one from a Big Book, the other the Good Book. The first is a piece on Acceptance from the Big Book of Alcoholics Anonymous (Pg 417 of the 4th edition) and the second a verse from Proverbs 3 of the Bible. [34]

The 12 steps were something I once balked at as I listened to them being discussed at those meetings my dad used to take me to and now they had turned my life around – they didn't do an awful lot for my career though.

3 *Alcoholics Anonymous* 4th edition (New York, AA World Services Inc, 2001) Pg 417
4 New King James Version: Proverbs 3: 5-6

CHAPTER 26

The Twelve Steps

A twelve-step program really amounts to nothing more than a spiritual journey, one that may look a fair bit different depending on one's perception of God (and there's wide spectrum, which can change an awful lot in the process). Ultimately it takes the focus from oneself, to that of others. Self-centeredness is at the root of most addictions, it's what led me to live a life like 'every day was New Years Eve'.

The twelve steps are structured in manner such that even someone as stubborn as me can succeed. All I really had to be able to do, aside from count from one to twelve, was to do the work. That's where the wheels can fall off, as the simplicity is mitigated by the fact that if one isn't willing to wholeheartedly and vigorously do the work and soul searching required, they may as well just abandon the whole idea and come back when they're ready.

The first seven steps involved making things right between myself and God, and the next two with making things right between myself and the rest of the world – neither of which I was capable of doing the first forty two years of my life. The last three steps simply help to improve upon the entire process while trying to change for the better, there isn't a finish line.

Growing up without a care in the world, I now found myself in that unfamiliar spot where I not only cared, but got involved. From being actively involved with service in my recovery program, in the community as a volunteer and very much involved in my church. These just weren't things one would have predicted years ago had they ventured to guess what I might have been doing in the future. It also left me with the pressing dilemma of what to do for living. After coming to the realization I had spent twenty-five years at an occupation which I wasn't even remotely interested in, and subsequently being fired, it was time to get on with that aspect of my life.

The MBA program in which I had enrolled wasn't one that I entered with any particular purpose in mind; as a matter of fact I couldn't say exactly what motivated me. Except perhaps that when once considering the idea and upon asking a former boss what he thought of the idea, he replied: "do you really think you're smart enough to get an MBA? You might want to try something different" – maybe the whole thing was out of spite. Regardless, there was no turning back now and besides, even I wasn't sure where to go with it, my grades were well above the average in the program, so that gave me a bit of confidence, something I had always lacked.

Finance was an area I did exceptionally well in, so it seemed the next logical career move might be that of a Financial Advisor. I was often getting inquiries along those lines but thought of responsibility frightened me. That's where recovery helped, as it's not so much about 'not drinking', rather far more about one's ability to deal with life – the lack of which is what caused the need to drink in the first place. Fear can be a large part of that; it always was for me and it was experienced again when considering career options. This time I had some practical experience to draw from.

A little earlier that year, the professor of an Entrepreneurial Finance course I was enrolled in, had asked if I would be part of a team of four to represent our school. It was a competition in Risk Management to be held at Dalhousie University in Halifax, one that would include teams from other MBA programs across the country. Each member had a specific role (we had an accountant, a techie, etc), and as the case was disclosed to us in stages, we would come up with a recommendation to present in front of a panel of professors. The professor had asked if I would fill the role of presenting our case and responding to questions from the panel – was he kidding?

Doing my best at hiding my thoughts, after saying I would consider it, a week was spent agonizing over the matter. Only a couple of years prior, I wouldn't have been able to stand in front of two people and read something off of a paper without my hand shaking to the point I couldn't read. Recovery and meetings had offered enough experience talking in front of people that I had overcome the fear to some extent – this would be different though. Way different. I finally came to the realization that the only way I was ever going to get past this was to take a risk and stop worrying about the outcome (and if I completely bombed, I probably wouldn't have been the first to do so).

That was the first real insight I had ever had into a much deeper issue, being the perplexing question as to discerning God's will. I had heard that concept of God's will mentioned again and again. In recovery, in worship, during sermons, in small groups, the only problem was, nowhere was I given a definitive answer as to where it could be found. I certainly didn't dispute the concept, I need only look at my own life and where running on self will had landed me – I couldn't run from it fast enough. God's will though, aside from some of the obvious spiritual principles like honesty, purity, love and unselfishness (the four absolutes that were part of the Oxford Group preceding AA), how could I find it on a personal level?

I needed simplicity and to have things spelled out for me – I wanted a neon sign flashing God's instructions. Here though, I sensed I might be on to something. To take a look at one thing I feared doing the most –there was a chance that perhaps that might be exactly what God was asking me to do. Considering I spent the better part of my life fearing pretty much everything, which basically stunted any development in the process, in all likelihood there would be no shortage of new fears arriving once I tackled the most pressing at hand. Thus became my new philosophy on determining what God's prompting might be. Not the most sound theological argument ever offered, or one that had religious precedent, but it was one that got me moving forward and starting to make decisions – that in itself was akin to moving mountains.

In this case, being part of that team and taking on the challenge of the competition was absolutely what I feared more than anything and the mere fact that I couldn't dismiss the thought was a pretty good indication in my mind that it was worth acting on – so I did. We had great weekend, enjoying Halifax immensely. I didn't self-destruct during the presentation, and our group even managed to reach the podium. Most importantly for me though, I had tackled one more fear head on. From that point forward it seemed to add to the armour required to deal with life on its own terms. Something I perhaps would have been well advised to have done years earlier – better late than never.

CHAPTER 27

Career Choices – Let's Push this Button

WITH the possibility of becoming a Financial Advisor the most practical option, along with the certainty that what I had been doing didn't appeal to me, I threw caution to the wind and headed down a new career path

I liked the idea of dealing with people; so this seemed like a step in the right direction, using my knowledge and helping others at the same time. Sales experience however, that wasn't an asset I brought to the table. In retrospect, that might have been something I ought to have considered before jumping in with both feet. Heck, I was never able to convince my dogs Tad or Buster to follow a simple command like 'sit', something that comes so naturally to a dog they would generally oblige most three year olds. If I couldn't sell a dog on what it should do instinctively, how was I going to be convincing with people who would be defensive from the start?

Maybe that should have served as a warning before engaging in a livelihood prefaced on the art of persuasion, like asking people to turn over their life savings for me to manage on their behalf. The commission only role I took on most definitely took convincing and hard-core sales skills. I worked at it though and gained the knowledge and experience I had to, even to the point of reaching a prescribed level to win a sales award one year – clinging closely to that adage that features tell and benefits sell. As much as it was a struggle, I thought perhaps there was a bit of hope for me yet.

Something was missing though; peers and colleagues seemed to have found their life purpose in helping families with goals and investments, but not me. So much of the industry was caught up in pushing profitable products, under the guise of financial plans personalized to meet one's individual goals. I was getting tired of listening to it, let alone trying to sell it. The products from one institution to another amounted to virtually the same thing; I didn't feel to be offering anything that someone couldn't get elsewhere. It had become more of a matter of trying to survive than a sense of actually helping anyone.

There was a gnawing emptiness in what I was doing, but I couldn't figure out what it was. Once upon a time it really wouldn't have mattered, but it did now. I also found it extremely difficult to target the most affluent in society; to do so is mandatory to some degree if one wants to succeed in a role as an advisor. The size of their book of business is the measuring stick by which to gauge their value to a firm –and to do so require some clients with significant wealth. Money just didn't hold as much importance to me as perhaps it should if I were to succeed, deep down in fact I felt if someone had three million dollars wanted to turn it into five, they probably had too much money to begin with.

That certainly didn't provide the facilitating motivation to gather the assets required to survive. Nonetheless I had to make a living doing something, all the while asking myself, *why can't you just settle for some success and leave it at that?*

God seemed to place into my heart a 'never just leave it at that' mentality though and it was beginning to get irritating. I would love to have settled for a period of just being stagnant. However, I had spent most of my life in a dormant state doing absolutely nothing and my memory wasn't so bad that I would forget where that got me. Even if it was kicking and screaming, I typically jumped into just about anything if given the slightest inking to do so.

The problem was, I never quite knew what I was getting into. I'd jump into something because it felt right, and then hope God would guide me along in the process. That's why forks weren't a deviation from the road at all for me, the only way I could view a road was in a rear view mirror. It had been that way with my decision to go back to school and it was that way now that I had made a career change. I thought there must be a reason for these avenues to open up before me; just wishing sometimes I had some kind of an idea where they led.

I was in complete and absolute awe of those who could devise step-by-step plans on how to approach a project and see it through to completion. Had I devised a six phase business plan (and the need to do so as an advisor was constantly drilled into my psyche) I wouldn't have made it half way through the second phase before the other four were rendered meaningless – everything would have changed. That's what my career felt like. Knowing what not to do was one thing, figuring out where to go, that felt like a task eternal.

CHAPTER 28

A Picture is worth a
Thousand Words

J UST when I would reach the point of frustration and wonder if the whole thing was a mistake, something always seemed to happen that offered some clarity. It was almost like God was giving instruction in small stages and too much at once might be overwhelming. My next breakthrough was to come after a trip to Nicaragua in the fall of 2008. This trip was to be one another of those things I intended to put off, but with increasing frequency I seemed to be being challenged by God on certain fronts – this being one of them. I was finding it increasingly difficult to ignore when it happened, which could be menacing. I might never have been in that mess had I not taken a course at that same church a couple of years earlier.

Kortright is a Presbyterian church in Guelph, not that I knew a great deal about the denomination when I started going and still don't actually – I couldn't tell you exactly what a Presbyterian is. Amongst the regulars at the church, it includes many who come from other denominations but find a sense of community there, as was the case with me, quite to my surprise. Aside from outreach and mission support, there's a strong focus on small groups and relationship building. That's quite different than what my perception of religion had always been and what I was brought up with. Alex, their new pastor after a significant period of looking for one, is a strong proponent as well and I wouldn't be surprised to see that church grow tremendously throughout the community in the next decade.

Several months sober I had decided to take an Alpha course there on the suggestion of my dear friend Kim. Her son was in the same class as Tim, and after dropping off our kids at St. Paul's in Guelph, many days we would spend time on the sidewalk outside of that small elementary school talking about life – she seemed like a woman touched by the hand of God. I had known her and her husband Jim prior to going to the Homewood and they were one of the few couples who didn't seem to feel awkward being around me in spite of my criminal charges, time in treatment, etc. It was during one of our chats sharing some of her own experience, she offered the Alpha suggestion.

I had heard of Alpha and although not convinced it was for me, it seemed like it might be worth trying. It's a course on the basics of the Christian faith, looking at the meaning of life from that perspective. I enjoyed the course right from the start, particularly the open environment that seemed unlike some church settings I had been around. No condemnation, no bias towards denominations, no need to be a Christian for that matter. If someone wanted to show up to observe and ask questions based on their unbelief that was okay too.

On the third or fourth lesson there was a teaching based on a piece of art. I wasn't exactly a connoisseur of art. In fact the only memory of my one visit to the Art Gallery in Toronto was waking up after falling asleep while standing and leaning on a display case. On that night at class though, there was something about that picture that was captivating and seemed to tell a compelling story – my own.

There was a man leisurely sitting in a chair glancing toward a door in front of him. On the other side of the door was a figure who was undoubtedly Jesus, yet He didn't enter the room – He couldn't. There was only one handle on the door and it was on the inside. I didn't have a clue who had painted it, but as I kept reflecting on the painting throughout the ensuing weeks, I was amazed that the artist had captured my entire existence in the brush of a few strokes. It was like looking at me firmly planted in that chair, which I had been throughout my life. During those years of questioning (my parents' divorce, my siblings illness), throughout the years of shame and guilt (my motorcycle accident and poor parenting), and through the years of addiction at its ugliest and the denial that accompanied it (I can do this on my own). My religious upbringing and belief in God weren't going to make one bit of difference because there was still one simple thing I would never do – get up and open the door.

It was the simple answer the entire time. I had remained firmly planted in that chair engaged in spiritual gymnastics, deliberating on the views of theologians and philosophers, all the time questioning God's existence and purpose. Why hadn't God done anything in my life? I almost laughed later as for the first time when I actually started reading the Bible that it was filled with stories of people who shared the same concerns as me. I just assumed that if you didn't have it all together and a rock solid faith to begin with, there was no point in opening that book at all.

I had always wondered where God was and now found it amazing to consider that He wanted in the whole time – I just wouldn't let Him. Once he did though, wow, at times it was almost overwhelming. It would be like sitting on the Maid of the Mist in the Niagara Gorge looking up at the fall's wondering "how do I turn off the tap". Which I could have done at anytime, but I was far too scared to close the door again. Between recovery programs and my church, I had built every safety net imaginable to keep that door wedged open.

I actually enjoyed it, as fellowship and actually talking to people about life was something I had never experienced before, certainly not in a church setting. In the days of my Catholic upbringing I would arrive at the last second and bolt before the processional hymn was done – generally straight to the pub. This was different;

I was amazed by the people, by their stories, and especially by their faith and how it affected the manner in which they lived.

I even started to read the Bible on occasion, which may not have been overly shocking to many people, but it sure was a step out in a new direction for me. With my upbringing, that's about the last thing you might have found me doing. I'll still tell people to this day that if you want to hide something from a Catholic, put in a Bible.

I can't really be critical though, that would simply be using the church as a scapegoat and laying blame elsewhere, which is something I used to love to do and was trying to get away from. It had far more to do with where I was at with my life than anything to do with the Church. There are an awful lot of amazing Catholics out there, and they have to be doing something right. I just happened to stumble on a place where religion seemed to come alive at the time I needed it. It was new to me and I wanted it to continue.

I even did a Step 5 (admitted to God, to ourselves and to another human being the exact nature of our wrongs) with a Catholic priest in my hometown, wanting to discuss at little bit about what I was going through. During course of our discussion and while telling him about my new experience at the church I had been attending, I couldn't help but feel at the time that a lecture was forthcoming.

Much to my astonishment, and something I point out to anyone who wants to be critical of Catholic priests and how close minded they are, that gentleman told me with complete sincerity to continue doing exactly what I had been. It was clearly doing me good. I was very proud of that priest for such honesty and heeded those wise words of instruction.

That led to a continued very strong connection with that church and relying heavily upon the several of the men I had become close to. Sobriety was great, but there was a growing desire to extend beyond a lifestyle that had become comfortable. The Nicaragua opportunity that presented itself would certainly stretch me beyond a point of comfort.

CHAPTER 29

Fruitful Labour (Nicaragua)

I had been asked to consider joining one of the teams in the past, but respectfully declined. I had always envisioned someone standing on a street corner rhyming off versus from the Bible – that just wasn't for me. A 'mission trip' was about the last thing I would ever do. Less than a year later, with the plane beginning its descent, I watched though the window and marvelled at the vast expense of lush green nestled amongst the volcanic mountains of Nicaragua.

Months earlier as we had been preparing, one of the guys pointed out to me that one of the biggest problems in Managua (the capital where they were headed) was alcoholism – they could use me on that trip. I didn't know much, but I knew a thing or two about alcoholism. I said I would think about it. Again, that gnawing feeling came back, the one that I've come to understand as being in a wrestling match with God – I've got a winless record in those matches.

All my life when challenged to try something new, I would put it off until I felt entirely ready. For all intents and purposes that resulted in never trying anything. For the Nicaragua trip, I had looked at the men going and considered how much more spiritual they were. I had no business being in their company, let alone joining in such a venture. Perhaps one day when I too would reach that level, then maybe I would consider it. I could have come up with a million excuses – it was all nonsense. This was the type of behaviour that working a recovery program had helped me to try and change. Half of those men were experiencing the same doubts I had.

When sensing trepidation because I feel ill equipped to do something, I now pay a lot of attention to that. More often than not, it's exactly where God wants to use me. Going on this trip, I had anything but the resources required – or so I thought. What I've since learned is that it's all part of the growth process and if I wait until I'm ready to do something, I'll probably never do it. It's a pretty radical approach to understanding God compared to what I grew up with and I've got a long way to go. However, something tells that if I don't, I'll miss out on the best that life has to offer. I eventually said yes to the Nicaragua team, and lacked absolutely nothing I wouldn't be given while there – excluding perhaps the ability to use a power gun.

With our view from window as the plane banked and began descending, it looked like we were arriving in paradise. Getting closer, fragments of that broken community would start to become apparent. Smoke rising from fires in the dumps surrounding Managua became visible, a setting that was home to hundreds who on a daily basis rely on its resources as a source for food and shelter. Appearances are deceiving though, and with all his preconceived notions, I was going to experience a different world over the course of those two weeks. The first notion to be dispelled was that of exactly what a mission trip is all about – these men impacted people in ways I never would have imagined. They second being who benefited the most from such a trip.

From a practical level, one purpose was to erect a structure that was to be used as a warehouse for PAN. It's a Non-Profit organization that was founded by a couple at Kortright and had been working in this country for the past decade. They had helped with churches, orphanages, schools and hospitals in the area and in so doing involved supplies donated from Canada that had to be stored until used. This warehouse would enable them to be far more efficient in serving the needs of that community.

Over the two-week period each morning was spent there, gradually watching it come closer to completion. To secure metal framing to structure, the fourteen men took turns imbedding the rivets into the metal frame with a few handguns on site. This included my contribution of a grand total of one rivet – which took me almost five minutes. My friend Charlie, slightly more capable at the procedure and a handyman by nature, patiently stood waiting and kind enough to refrain from offering his opinion until I had finished.

"That's good enough Dan, why don't you help with the trenches". We were also digging to lay piping for the septic tank to be installed – I wasn't allowed near that gun for the remaining two weeks. My wife Sian found it difficult to believe when I first shared that story. After nine months of marriage and gaining a clearer understanding of my abilities, or lack thereof, she would now concur with Charlie that a single rivet was indeed one too many.

The warehouse task was important, but not what left a lasting impression. At first it was very simple things, like visiting a small church in a run-down barrio (what we would refer to as a neighbourhood) that the youth from our church had helped build a couple of years earlier. Walking the streets, I experienced a sense of community unlike any I had seen before. Kids were out on the streets kicking cans and playing games with their neighbours, even their brothers and sisters. At the same time, back home kids the same age were often in separate rooms on their own computers occupied on MSN or Facebook – family was nowhere in sight.

In that same barrio on a daily basis we helped create additional resources for a sports ministry that PAN had established. This entailed turning an overgrown garbage infested wasteland into a sports field. Aside from being attacked by red ants as we used machetes to remove the waist high weeds littered with condoms, tampons and used needles, what I remember most was the parents coming to watch and be overjoyed to see us take an interest in their community. The kids would appear out of nowhere the second we arrived each day.

Many of them were around the same age as my kids – they wanted to see pictures, they wanted to hear stories. The likes of Christiana, Lilia, Solana – a group of ten year olds who I would have taken home if I could. Not only were they were adorable, until Doug walked by and made a comment, I thought they liked me well. "Hey Dan, you do realize the only reason they like you is because you have a pink camera." My bubble was temporarily burst and I immediately tried to recall how I came about having this camera. It was the evening before I left.

"Tim, can I borrow your camera?" "Well dad, mine doesn't work so well, best try one of the girls" he responded.

"Sorry dad", Shae Lynn piped up before even being asked, as she saw the question coming. "I've got a field trip while you're gone, so I'm going to need it."

"Amber, what about you, can I use yours?"

Needless to say, they knew me well enough and simply didn't trust me with anything valuable of theirs – I had a tendency to be a little clumsy. Nor did I have a clue how to use a digital camera, so they were even more protective. Without even having to resort to a bribe, Amber was finally gracious enough to say sure; she would let me use hers. I paid very little notice to the camera at time, as she briefly described how it worked, besides she correctly pointed out, someone would be able to help me anyway.

All the guys had cameras and we would share the pictures later, so I had barely touched mine at that point of our trip. With these kids though, I had made sure to bring mine that day as they loved to take pictures of each other, then quickly huddle together and giggle while immediately viewing them. That's what the girls were doing as they had surrounded me that morning, while I beamed at the attention.

Doug was right, it really was pink. Worse yet, those girls only liked me for my camera – I was heartbroken. From that moment forward, for the rest of the trip I was self-conscious whenever it was

DAN MATWEY

visible. First chic flicks and now a pink camera – maybe I should be getting concerned.

Doug was kidding and reassured me it had nothing (or at least little) to do with my camera. It took a while to be convinced, but was a relief to hear. All was forgiven, not that I had much choice; otherwise I would be in search of a new interpreter. He was one of those guys who had actually committed some time and effort preparing to learn a bit of Spanish in advance of leaving. By the end of the trip, along with a few others, he could have broken conversations with the locals in their own language. I on the other hand, had an exam the night before leaving and spent a full hour at 2am the morning we left listening to a CD my friend Jim had given me. I figured that should provide a solid foundation upon which to build and four hours later as our plane took off; I knew roughly eight words in Spanish. Two weeks later when we returned, after being thoroughly confused, I came home knowing fewer than when I left. There were a couple of official interpreters, but they were always in high demand, so for simple conversations with the kids, I needed those other guys who had prepared a little better than me.

We made progress on the sports field every day, to the point where goal posts had been cemented in and it was ready for use. On our last day visiting that site, we watched a soccer tournament take place with hundreds of kids participating. The children of that barrio had reclaimed a field that was rightfully theirs. Whether or not there would be help in taking the initiative to maintain it was the only question that remained. Hopefully they would take ownership and pride in that field so that it could continue to serve for the purpose it was intended – but that was beyond our control and probably better left for God to deal with.

Over the course of our stay we also visited orphanages, hospitals and feeding centers. This is where I found us to have the greatest influence, giving me a much stronger sense of the value of mission trips. It had nothing to do with construction, cleaning up a mess or enabling (which skeptics will accuse teams of doing) – it was all about relationship. A far cry from the impression I had of standing on a street corner reciting bible verses, what we recited instead were our own stories, while hearing theirs. The Nicaraguans took great delight in the fact someone would just spend the time talking and listening.

I will always recall how with complete amazement, the local residents watched as foreigners engaged in their community. No doubt it was a rare occurrence, particularly with so many father's being absent from their families, almost to the point of epidemic proportions. In some instances it was simply a case where the man of the home was only capable of finding employment in another city, in many cases it was a matter of abandonment, or neglect as a result of addiction.

There's a special moment that will remain indelibly etched in my mind and it was completely unplanned, as quite often the most memorable of occasions are. Actually, to this day, whenever I consider a weekend retreat, conference, or anything of that sort, Christian event or otherwise (and I enjoy those as well), the very first thing I'll look at is the agenda and just how structured it is. If it's planned to the precise detail, I would rather not attend. Sure, there can be great speakers, great lessons taught, great everything, but there's absolutely no room left for God to show up in an unexpected fashion and I find that to be the best part of all.

It sure was on that day, when a spontaneous baseball game against a group of local teenagers meant anything but a manner of filling idle time. We had travelled to another barrio for a scheduled baseball game against a Nicaragua national club entitled the 'one arm bandits'. Quite literally, this was a team comprised of men who had lost an arm at some point in their life and they played competitively against other teams with men having a similar disability. Our opponents were late in arriving that day ('Nicaraguan time' is the phrase used to explain that very common occurrence), but there had been room left on the schedule to allow for it. It's also why the most important part of the day was even given an opportunity to develop.

While waiting and throwing the ball around amongst each other, one by one some local teenagers started to come by. They were doing the same in a separate part of the diamond, when with very little ability to communicate; the two groups eventually came to the understanding we would have some fun game against each other while waiting for our scheduled opponent. Without enough equipment to go around, gloves and bats were shared after switching between taking to the field or the plate.

It was an antiquated park, definitely constructed for baseball as there were concrete benches that acted as the stands. At one point in time they might have been well occupied – on this day they would be once more. While both teams, in a boisterous fashion with plenty laughing and hollering, continued with our game, those seats gradually began to fill throughout the course of the next half hour. Word had spread and people were coming to watch must have been an extremely rare site of grown men playing with their sons – the smiles were priceless. The mere fact that it randomly occurred made it that much more special.

In terms of the ball game, those kids were more gracious than they had to be, going out of their way to ensure their elderly guests didn't look so bad. As kind as they were in that respect, they were even more appreciative. No words had to be said for the message to clearly come across that they knew they were involved in something very special.

As for the 'one armed bandits', they did show up a little later and proceeded to place a thumping on their Canadian guests. After being taught a lesson or two that day, I realized what the problem had been all those years and why I was such a poor ballplayer – I had one too many arms.

As important as relationship was with those in the country we were visiting, those that developed within our team was of equal importance. We started off as a group of fourteen men, most of who knew each other as an acquaintance, but very little beyond that. Over the course of two weeks that began to change. Our sleeping quarters consisted of a couple of adjoining rooms similar to a small residence, with ten or so beds in each room. The section in front of both rooms was joined by an extended porch, which wasn't always vacant, even if we were gone. We had a frequent visitor. If there were two things I once might have once sworn would never happen in my lifetime, along with 'go on a mission trip', might have been the words 'get within a foot of a Tarantula' – now I had done both. With its striking appearance and magnificent colors I was enthralled, actually a bit disappointed those few nights that it wasn't present.

Each evening we spent a couple of hours having 'porch time' as previous men's trip had referred to it, and the first few were simply spent reflecting on our day and unloading whatever was weighing on us, a result of being exposed to new culture. Those nights would typically start off with some well played, but poorly sung music. We were fortunate enough to have Brian, an immensely gifted member of a church worship team having joined us for the trip. With him finding out half way through the trip that his leadership skills in other areas were as big an asset to the team as his musical talents, it exemplified a serendipitous aspect to this trip. Many men unexpectedly even learned something about themselves while they were there.

After opening with music and a bit of prayer each evening, it would be followed by some conversation that could take on varying degrees of intensity depending on the type of day we had. Within fairly short order, the routine turned into one where each night a different member of the team would spend some time-sharing their story – we all have one and they carry a lot of power when honestly shared.

As the days went by and the feeling of safety and level of trust increased, between the stories themselves and the ensuing conversations that resulted, there was far more vulnerability that prevailed. It was amazing to watch and something I wouldn't have traded for anything. It was quite clear that some men were beginning to share things they had never told anyone in their life and healing was beginning to take place. At times it was done in group, other times one on one, as there was ample opportunity for that. Disguises were shed and the group began to expose themselves for whatever brokenness they carried (even those who had the stories that seemed so ideal on the surface). These were all men for whom life wasn't perfect and there had been struggles – I thought I was the only one. It was incredible gift that came from that fourteen day journey and to this day, three years later, you can pretty well tell at that church the men who formed that team, simply by a bond that was created spending time on the porch.

There was one final aspect of the trip that was of such significance and it remains my dream to one day go back and be able to continue what was started. It's also the reason I went in the first place. As I was told before going, alcoholism was a major problem where we were visiting. This was an area where I hoped to be of help and began to prepare right after confirming with the group I would be joining their team.

My friend Jim was of immense help in that preparation. Jim is a quiet leader, a man with a tremendous passion for self-development, particularly in a church environment where so often it's easy to sit back and simply adapt to programs. He had been the discipleship pastor at Kortright when I took that Alpha course, is a man I have great respect for and has been like a mentor to me ever since that time. He's also fluent in Spanish and led me through several conversations with a pastor local to the barrio we would be going. He had identified some men who were suffering with their addiction issues and see if they would allow me to see them. To whatever extent possible, he was going to communicate with these men that

I was an alcoholic who was once in as bad, if not worse shape than they were.

Armed with my own experience, along with several Spanish copies of AA's Big Book, I was ready to tackle the task. This would be something to do on my own, and the group was fully appreciative that it might be a little intimidating for those men to see our entire entourage appear at the front door.

The first week was somewhat disappointing, never really having the opportunity to meet up with any of the men I had hoped. However, something far more valuable, yet unexpected occurred. I used to laugh at the notion that one's plans might be interrupted because God could have better ones; I'm no longer the cynic I was.

I went through the barrio with Manuel that first week. He was an official interpreter, a diminutive man with a great sense of humor and tremendous spirit. Although none of the men were available, I did get a chance to spend time talking to their spouses and kids. I hadn't thought of it before leaving, but early into those discussions realized how important it was for them to hear my story. They were under the impression that if they would only love their husband's or father's more, than perhaps he wouldn't drink so much – somehow they viewed it as their fault.

I shared what it was like growing up in an alcoholic home, as well as what I was like when active in my addiction and how my own kids suffered. I was absolutely no different than those men were. I talked to them about the illness that addiction is and how it affects everyone in the family. What they walked away with was an understanding for the first time of the fact that they were dealing with somebody in their family who was sick and that his drinking had nothing to do with anything that they as a wife or a child did or did not do. Nor did it mean they weren't loved, speaking at length of my own desire to love, but inability to do so when I was ill. It had changed for me and I was now better and they now had hope that the same could happen in their families.

The next week I did meet with many of the men as planned by that pastor. To my amazement, they would openly invite me to enter whatever semblance of a home that they had and offer a place to sit. I walked through portions of the book I brought and left for them. As I used my English version, and they the Spanish one, through the interpreter I would share my own experience.

I wasn't shy about telling them what God had done in my life and the circumstances that led to becoming sober. I couldn't help but be amused at their justification for drinking. There is something universal about an addiction whereby there's always an excuse to justify one's behaviour. There's always that one thing that will make a situation unique, such that nobody else could possibly relate to what you're going through – I had lived that lie longer than I cared to remember. Hearing their excuses was like listening to my voice from years gone by. It sure made it easy to respond, almost like being in a poker match and saying "I'll match your excuse and raise you one".

Did it do any good? Maybe, maybe not, that would be up to them to determine. I did all I could, even if nothing more than to plant a seed. That's the least I could do, considering what others had once done for me.

CHAPTER 30

A Foot in both Worlds

Upon returning and being back on Canadian soil, the astounding part of it all was not that I had been involved in the experience of a lifetime, rather the reason why – because I drank too much. As a result of my miserable past, some thought I could be of value to the team. Only in God's world is that possible.

As ludicrous and impractical as I once might have thought some of those stories out of the Old Testament to be, when I now see a phrase like "I will reclaim the years the locust has eaten" – I don't question it anymore. In fact I think, *I wonder what else I should be paying attention to.*

After coming home, I also began to seriously question many aspects of the culture I was coming back to. I was told that could happen and to be prepared for it, but still didn't expect it to affect me – it occurred quickly. Not even one full day after returning, it all seemed to be put into perspective while watching the news. At a Wal-Mart in the US an employee was killed by stampede of Christmas shoppers as the doors opened on black Friday.

Was this really what I wanted to come home to? A culture so consumed in their over indulgence it will feed behaviour that will border on being insane. I was going to see it throughout the rest of the Christmas season as well, watching the pandemonium that was about to transpire at the local malls as it did every year. All the while, our world would look at an underdeveloped nation such as that of Nicaragua and feel sorry for them. They lack so much, if only they could be more like us – now that's insane.

At the same time, I returned to a state of panic such that one would have thought the Western world as we knew it was coming to an end. The stock markets around the globe were in the midst of a free fall the likes of which hadn't been seen in decades. If working in the industry had taught me anything, it was simply the confirmation of the extent to which people base their identity on how much money they have. If their portfolios disappeared, what was left of them? Evidently nothing, judging by what I read. No wonder people jumped out of windows during the mother of all crashes in 1929. I wondered if this time it would be different, would there be emergency staff lining the sidewalks with safety nets, or by some miracle might some good come as a result of it?

Maybe the fact that there was no money would force people to stay at home instead of going out to a restaurant for dinner – they might have to spend time together as a family. Perhaps as a family cost cutting measure, some of those computers would have to be sacrificed, the ones with the kids chained to them serving no other purpose than to keep them isolated. Then brothers and sisters here may actually have to play with one another as well, like they do in those countries we feel sorry for.

It actually made working as a Financial Advisor extremely challenging when I came back. After experiencing everything I had, only to come home and witness everything that was going on here at the same time, I felt like I had a foot in two different worlds. With clients being alarmed, I had the standard corporate reply at my fingertips to ease their blood pressure; "don't panic, you're in this for the long haul. This has happened before and we've got a plan in place to withstand it" … blah, blah, blah.

I was convinced there was always a great opportunity that could prevail from something that looked so dismal on the surface. What I really wanted to tell my clients who felt like all was lost was a somewhat different response than the industry standard. I simply wanted to scream as loud as I could, "shut up, open your eyes and take stock of what is important." I couldn't though, I might get fired.

In the meantime, Nicaragua wasn't quite experiencing the same sense of panic, and my thoughts kept drifting back there. Theirs was a culture immune to the greed fanning a fire that would ultimately cause our system to collapse upon itself with the mortgage meltdown we went through. To them, subprime loans were a lost language; Bear Stearns; Fannie Mae and Freddy Mac might be characters in a Hollywood production they would never see. They wouldn't know the difference between a hedge fund from a mulberry bush, nor would they have desire to learn. They had nothing to lose because they never had anything to begin with – except a freedom in spirit. For all they lacked, there was something they did have, something that circumstances like a free falling market or pending recession weren't about to change. They relied on each other and on their faith – and they were happy. I was beginning to get some clearer insight as to why Pierre Burton and Mother Teresa saw things so differently in Calcutta – exclude God from the picture and things can look dark in an awful hurry.

In the meantime, I had a job to do. Everyone else at the office was excited about the potential that would result from portfolio values that were falling by the minute. People would panic, they would be scared, they would be angry – they would need someone to blame. Therein lay the golden opportunity; it was a great time to be in the business. Simply be a consoling voice to those disgruntled clients of the competitor, listen with empathy as they described their disappointment over their advisor's lack of foresight – become their beacon of hope.

In the meantime, as one's own clients were going through precisely the same thing, the trick was being sensible enough to console and try and salvage their business. Keep your own and go out with guns blazing to get as many as possible and move their assets over before things got better. The corporate message to deliver was along the lines of 'I would never have created the mess your advisor has gotten you into". Convince them of that and they would all line up like sitting ducks – this job wasn't really doing much for me anymore.

CHAPTER 31

The Next Job Loss

JOHN Bunyan, an outspoken preacher of the 17th century who wrote Pilgrim's Progress during the period his incarceration once said "if my life is fruitless, it doesn't matter who praises me. If my life is fruitful, it doesn't matter who criticizes me".

I was working in an industry which plenty of people made ridiculous amounts of money and received accolades galore. I suppose the goal had always been to become one of them, but there was a lack of desire to do so – even with the incentives to motivate me. Praise was the pinnacle sign of success, but the work felt fruitless.

Nicaragua had been an experience where there was no monetary reward, and nobody was measuring my success as compared to others with bi-weekly reports for all to see. It was just me and the situations I encountered – God challenging me with what I would do. Now that was fruitful. And confusing, because now what was I supposed to do? That was the million-dollar question. Once again, I found myself in that familiar position where I didn't have a clue why I was doing what I was doing. Then the path became clear – I thought.

In the spring of 2007 the Canadian Federal Government announced the creation of a new program designed specifically to help individuals challenged by some form of disability. The Registered Disability Savings Plan finally launched in December of 2008 after being announced in the federal budget the previous spring, and I followed its progress with extreme interest. I was barely back from my trip and the timing seemed perfect to start preparing for a change within the industry.

Finally I had found that niche area of the industry I had been looking for. This was a particular demographic with which I had great empathy and understood the emotional turmoil it caused families because of what our family had been through. I was keenly aware of the fact that if done properly, alleviating some of the financial concerns would improve an already overly stressful life. As such, once again I was changing jobs, this time voluntarily as opposed to being summoned into an office for a conversation that was always prefaced with "Dan, I'm sorry we have to ... "

Here I would be working with a full service brokerage firm. With a licence to sell securities, for the first time I would have the investment universe at his fingertips. I thought that was pretty cool – it made me feel important. For any investment portfolio of significant value it provided for far superior alternatives to one limited to Mutual Funds, as had been the case previously. That was something I welcomed, however it wasn't the primary reason for moving.

My new firm was the brokerage arm of the first institution to carry the RDSP and I wanted to leverage off of the commitment of that bank. It seemed like a great fit, as I had been a strong advocate of this new plan for many reasons. After age and income restrictions (it wasn't perfect, but no other country in the world had such an initiative) were taken into account, for a great many disabled Canadians the government grants tied to matching contributions was staggering. With $4,500 annually being added to a $1,500 contribution, that $6,000 maximized each year over a twenty year period created an unprecedented ability for caregivers to ensure a loved one was financially stable after they were gone. What was once a pipe dream had become a reality because most important of all, any assets held and income generated by the plan would be completely exempt from affecting government programs (Ontario Disability Support Payments primarily) already in place. That was critical and made it all that much more attractive. It was a message I wanted to get out to families.

That coupled with the intricate estate planning strategies they could adopt, and there would be tremendous value to be gained. From tax and insurance strategies, Henson Trusts to further protect the beneficiary to third party trustees to facilitate the process, there was so much potential that I was excited to finally have a purpose within the industry. This was my dream, my passion and truly the one area where I knew with certainty that I had more to offer than other advisors in the industry. That insecurity which plagued me all my life was gone. Unlike twenty-five years ago, I would no longer place my fate in the hands of someone who didn't even know me.

I started presenting seminars, I wrote articles, and after a period of time I had organizations contacting me to come and speak to their membership. I had others asking me to come and speak to their staff – the referrals and subsequent business would be staggering. Families could strongly identify with my personal stories, and I gladly shared them. Incidents like when his brother had recently been duct taped to a pole by a bunch of teenagers at a high school across the street from my mother's house. A guy who was formerly an all star hockey player in Junior, one that would willingly drop his gloves if need be and generally pummel whoever got out of hand – now frail and thirty pounds lighter, he would be targeted by teenagers because of his vulnerable state and appearance. After hearing that story I was livid. I thought justice should have been served and if I was in a position to do so, likely would have unleashed a flurry of vengeance myself.

My brother's reaction was slightly different. "They're teenagers; do they really have any idea what they're doing?" I likely learned more about forgiveness on that occasion than any other in my life.

I would tell parents what that meant to estate planning, by repeating what I had told my own mother. I didn't want to be the guy that handled my brother and sister's money after she was gone

– it would create too much friction. That's what happens with a Henson Trust, someone needs full discretion over the finances and it can't be the individual with the disability. Parents typically look to the healthy member of a family to do so. It places an inordinate amount of stress on the family dynamic. I simply wanted to be a brother and that was it. So my mom changed her will and altered her plans – she felt much better after doing so.

Families at seminars loved to hear these types of things; it resonated with what they were going through in their own lives. More organizations and people continued to contact me and it was all coming together, minus one vital piece – it wasn't generating any business. There would be no salary attached to my role once training was done, so that was a critical missing element.

My manager had warned me of the risk in becoming specialized and the time it would take to succeed – I marched ahead anyway. Colleagues discussed the risk of seminars being a great source for educating people, but doing little to actually get traction business wise – I marched ahead anyway. After a period of time, I was beginning to sense that people were using me to gain information they wouldn't otherwise receive and were grateful for it. At the same time, they maintained relationships with their current advisors – but I marched ahead anyway.

With my personal experience, education, my interest and knowledge in this field – the stars were perfectly aligned and I was certain it was my turn. I would be the most trusted advisor in the industry with families facing such issues. All those years of doing an MBA, being in an industry that I wasn't really sure why I was there – now it was all making sense. This was the path God had wanted me on all along, and if God were with me, who could be against me?

Well, my manager for one. Which I found out when those familiar words were softly spoken once more and I was requested to close the door and come in for a meeting. "Things don't seem to be working out the way you had planned Dan, and I know you've given it everything you could, but I think it's time you realize this position is really not for you".

To his credit, I was given several weeks time to prepare for the transition, his most immediate concern being that I didn't just walk out the door with nowhere to go – that wasn't necessary, but was certainly appreciated. And with that, after all my years of drinking and never being fired, once again, while in recovery and being sober I found myself being dismissed.

I hadn't had an awful lot of dreams in my life, so to have one such as this shattered definitely hurt. I was lost as to what to do and was none too pleased with God either. However, unlike other times in my life, drinking wasn't the solution – it couldn't be. Those two pieces I liked to read helped. That bit on Acceptance as well as Proverbs 3, because my own understanding wasn't going to explain this one. I was beginning to get a better sense of just how admirable a man like Job really was – I read that book again as well. Ultimately, turning back to God was the only place to go for an answer, because as much as I didn't understand the reasoning behind what happened, based on the other truths of my life, God was about the only certainty I had. Amidst the turbulence, there was a lot of reassurance in that.

After a period of time, as I reflected on the experience and on what I had been trying to do and why it failed, I was able gain a little more clarity – and extend myself a little grace at the same time. My sponsor Bobby reminds me to do that and I'm glad he does. Maybe I wasn't the failure I thought I was. As important as some of the financial issues facing these families were, and those opportunities would remain, I began to understand that many were facing much greater issues.

Shame and guilt, dealing with social stigma and stereotype – these were far more paralyzing than those financial matters I was trying to address. I had seen their eyes lit up as I spoke about some of financial strategies available and what could be achieved, but

DAN MATWEY

at the same time I saw their sorrow as I probed a little deeper and uncovered the truth. The primary reason why none of these things had been implemented by current advisors, accountants, or lawyers, was that in many instances, those professionals hadn't the slightest idea that disability was even an issue in the family. Many people (certainly not all) didn't want them to know, that would have been exposing those self-perceived flaws.

That entire failed experiment did nothing for my career, but sure offered some unexpected insight. The irony of what I was able to witness was that it wasn't so much the disabled kids who were in need of help at all – the programs that have been developed over the past few decades have left them light years ahead of where they once might have been. Parents, siblings and grandparents though, that was quite often entirely different. It reminded me of that story of the puppies who walked just like their paralyzed mother because it's all they had seen and been exposed do. Many of these folks were denying themselves of a new freedom they had no idea was at their disposal, and some of the secrets, shame and guilt they carted around with them was toxic.

I wished I could get a bus (a really big bus), round them all up and cart them off to Celebrate Recovery. That's a Christian based twelve-step program, not unlike Alcoholics Anonymous. Lakeside church in Guelph (where Sian and I were married) is a large community Christian Church that places a large emphasis on community and healing. They have one of the largest Celebrate Recovery programs in the province, one which I've been active in for the past couple of years. Instead of limiting itself to addictions however, it helps people deal with hurts and hang-ups of any variety. Seeing people come from broken marriages, deal with abuse issues as a child, address their co-dependent, people pleasing, or control issues; I loved to see the freedom that could be found when people surrendered this baggage from their past and allowed God to do some work in their life.

I thought these families could desperately use something like that, but had to remember I was a financial advisor and not a therapist. Maybe that was my problem all along and I was just in the wrong occupation – my career dilemma was getting more confusing all the time.

CHAPTER 32

And then there were Three

"So here's what I think dear." I wasn't even married yet, but she was sharing her opinions anyway, solicited or otherwise. Within a few months after we would be married, I would hear her thoughts even more frequently, but I loved that about Sian. We actually discussed everything – it was part of the deal. I had gotten to the point where I valued and wanted to know what she thought – even if I didn't always agree with it (more often than not, I would come around to her way of thinking anyway).

On that specific day, it was all related to career and after the recent job loss and us about to be married in two months; there was a lot of discussion as to what I should do. One option was to continue to follow my passion, simply hook up with a new firm and rely on a sudden flurry of sales activity when none had occurred in the past. That would either require a tremendous leap of faith, or a large degree of stupidity, I wasn't sure which. Those neon signs I wished that God would use to point me in the right direction – I think all the bulbs needed replaced because I couldn't see them.

Alternatively, I could look for stability, something with benefits, a pension, and most importantly a paycheck I could rely on every couple of weeks. It had been years since being in such a spot, almost as far back as my drinking days.

"Why don't you do something safe and when I get back to work, then you should follow your dream", suggested my wife to be. She had run her own charity up until a few years prior, at which point aside from moving to Guelph with her daughter Cati, spent a year with her mother as she was dying. After finally being ready to get back into the work force, she was rear ended in an accident a few blocks from her home, which set her back once more. Sian was on the mend and making progress, but it would be a few months yet before she was in the position to work on a regular basis. That left us in a vulnerable position and it seemed like the secure route might be the prudent thing to do. There was an offer on the table and I had to make a decision.

So, as a financial advisor with several years in the industry, I decided to change roles and take the secure route a bank had to offer. I would have to forfeit my license to sell insurance, as well as lose the ability to purchase individual stocks and bonds as mandated in a bank advisory role, but for the sake of my bride, I went ahead and took one for the family. For good reason as well, roles that offer as much job security as a bank are few and far between. As a friend and colleague claimed when I started, 'it's almost impossible to get fired from a bank. You would be more likely to have failed kindergarten."

It may not have been my dream job, but how much of sacrifice was it anyway? Even if the role did seem a little mundane, my ascent up the corporate ladder was soon to follow. God must have taken away my previous role for a reason and this had become available for another – in time it would be clear what the reason might be. I was excited, not so much about the job I was starting; rather where it might lead down the road (the unemployment line wasn't exactly the first thing that came to mind).

So, in mid November with Christmas and a New Years Eve wedding on the horizon, off I went to start my new role. Working from nine until five, and having evenings and weekends free, this was a luxury I hadn't experienced in years. So what if it was me and fourteen women at the branch, if that was my biggest challenge then so be it. It wasn't my biggest challenge – if anything it was the position's most redeeming quality.

"Mutual Funds are stupid. The stock market's fixed and don't you dare try and make me lose all my money", he said, while taking a seat opposite me without the meeting having even gotten under way. *Okay, that's very nice; thanks for being so candid and sharing your concerns,* I thought, hoping this might just be an anomaly. I just wished I had the opportunity to introduce myself before being subjected to the tirade.

"Sir, the fees are too high on my account. I don't think banks should be charging me to let them hold my money. You should feel ashamed of yourself." I wasn't aware that acting as the corporate complaint department was part of the job description, but I was getting used to this.

"What's the best you can get us on a 5 year GIC? Your posted rate is ridiculous. Do you want us to go down the street and see what they'll offer?" Actually, yes I did want them to go down the street – and more than that I wished they would stay there. Not just those two, there were plenty more that could accompany them.

"Aren't you a little old to be doing this job?" Okay that's it I thought, shaking my head. *Somebody shoot me – please!!!*

Such were the nature of many of the conversations I had on any given day. Sure, there were some nice people, there were those who it was a delight to serve and there might even have been the odd financial planning discussions now and again, but they were few and far between. I was beginning to sense that the bank client was an entirely different breed than what I had expected, certainly than what I was accustomed to. I had broad shoulders though and their bickering wasn't going to get to me.

Procedures and expectations within the bank setting though, that was an entirely different matter. From securing vault codes and verifying information to the point of ad nauseam, to understanding the multitude of accounts and their features – there wasn't a teller alive who wouldn't have been better at that than me. Administrative and advisory skills were not one and the same and where I fell woefully short was in the one I was being asked to excel at.

If someone showed up with half a million dollars and wanted some ideas on what to do with it, I could have a pretty good discussion. However if little Johnny's mom had five minutes to spare and came barging in demanding her son have his own account, with a shiny can, because Billy next door kept bragging about his own – then I would look like a deer lost in the headlights. It was Johnny's mom far more than the prospective investor who most frequently walked through the door.

In terms of investment sales, I was actually doing quite well, periodically having some outstanding results. The most rewarding aspect of my role came during those rare discussions with people who were seriously looking at specific goals or other aspects of their financial plan. They thanked me for a level of discussion many acknowledged they had never before experienced at a bank. That made me feel worthwhile, it's what I enjoyed, and that's the experience I wanted more customers to walk away with. It's what I considered to be the most valuable asset I could off to my employer – it's also what the bank had the least interest in.

They wanted products sold, not plans laid out. Plans weren't profitable and they were time consuming, even if most did market themselves around the intense planning they would do for their customers. Products are what fed the bottom line, leaving me in a quandary to say the least. If such products would fit a client's need, I would have no problem selling them, but if they didn't, then I had an issue on my hands.

Protection of assets and income for example are an integral part of financial planning, but doing so a in a comprehensive and cost effective manner is equally important. Being formerly licensed to sell and insurance, I was well aware that there were far more suitable options than what a bank had to offer. With the disproportion between its cost and the value it offered, mortgage and credit insurance were extremely profitable to a bank, but generally a poor fit for the consumer. I had a hard time accepting the cleverly designed approach to convincing clients it's something they really needed.

That familiar sense of impending doom was beginning to rear its ugly head once again. I did what I could and focused on where I knew my strengths to be, but ultimately fought a losing battle. Ah, if only I were still drinking, then I could have cared less what I sold people or whether or not it was good for them. As long as it satisfied my own needs, that would have been good enough for me.

On the last day at that job, I had the most successful of any in my seven months with the firm. I had just secured the most significant transfer of assets into our branch in quite some time. This was a result of discussions I had been having over the preceding few weeks, updating management on the status regularly as requested. Those transfers were a result of the rapport I had already developed, along with the ongoing relationship those clients anticipated in the future. To wait until the moment of confirmation and then pull the plug – that just wasn't right. Not so much for me, I was evidently on life support anyway, but that' s no way to treat real people with real money who aren't aware their decisions are being made under false pretences. It's the only thing that didn't sit well with me as I left, however, that would have to be on the conscience of someone else – it wasn't my burden to carry.

I had done my best and couldn't argue with the manager's decision. I wasn't a good fit for that branch. So in spite of what my friend had told me when I started there, I simply took the news that day, said thanks for the opportunity and walked out the door as the latest, in fact the first and only that I was aware, kindergarten failure.

The ride home was one in which the only thing I worried about was how others would take the news. My wife would be disappointed for me, after all, who likes to see someone rejected, but would encourage me to remain positive. She would stress about money for all of 14 seconds and completely turn her thoughts elsewhere. Whenever she does have any money, she just gives it away to someone she thinks needs it more anyway. Finally, since I found it increasingly painful just to go to work for those previous few months anyhow, she would reassure me that is was all for the best. It was high time I did something I enjoyed and in the meantime, a few home cooked meals would be nice for a change. So Sian I wasn't overly concerned about.

I was more worried about my mother. She was from a generation where it was all about pensions and security and had desperately hoped this was where I would find that. Having had a front row seat to the debacle of which I had made of my life, the biggest fear for her might be that it would set me off and back to my former ways. All things considered, I could understand where such concern might come from, however that would be for her to deal with – nothing positive would come from me worrying about her reaction. There was nothing that God wasn't stronger than anyway. I knew that, and was also aware that setbacks usually forced me to increase my reliance on God even more. Perhaps this would be good for me in the long run. My mom would see in time that I wouldn't self-destruct over this, so she would be okay too.

I was probably most concerned about sharing what happened with my friend and colleague Julie – she had referred me to the position in the first place. Aside from her help there, she was almost single handily responsible for bringing Sian and I together as well.

After having known each other for a couple of years through that singles group at Lakeside church, in spite of my best failed efforts, I had long given up any hope of ever taking Sian on a date. We had spent time with each other at various activities, having had the occasional conversation, but that looked like the extent to which we would know one another. There were three and half billion other women on the planet who weren't overly interested in getting to know me, this would only be one more added to the list – I didn't take it too personally.

In June of 2010, at a church related group we both attended, Sian was sharing how her mom had recently passed away after a long bout with cancer. She expressed her gratitude to the women of that church who had been so supportive in helping her throughout the ordeal. I meant to offer my condolences later that evening but got sidetracked and the next day at work, felt bad that I hadn't done so. Without knowing Sian's email or number, I sent a note to Julie asking her to pass along my condolences if she saw her.

Having left it at that, with the following day being a holiday, I returned back to work a couple of days later seeing an email from Sian. Not immediately recognizing the name, my initial thought was that perhaps is was some new business – that excited me. Those were the days of my seminars, which always resulted in a fair degree of response and I was at the point of needing a miracle to survive in that position. After thinking about it a little more I realized who it was from, I only knew one woman named Sian and then remembered the message I had given Julie.

I was so nervous it took me ten minutes to open the email, at which time I expected to see something along the lines of "thanks for your thoughts, that was very nice". Instead there were several paragraphs and immediately it was closed – I was way too nervous to read it.

Twenty minutes later, mustering up the gumption, I went on to read how Julie had passed along my condolences to Sian, at the same time suggesting she should go out for a coffee with me. She had said I was actually a pretty nice guy if she got to know me. Sian, out of curiosity went on to read the bio on my business website and in her note to me commented on her surprise at the many things we had in common. That was all I had to hear and having already put myself through enough torture that morning, didn't see any harm in taking the risk and asking her out dinner. The door had been opened; I may never get another chance. Planning to go for an hour or so, we went out that evening and spent hours talking at a restaurant – the rest is history.

So, although concerned about my well-being, Julie knew I had a supportive wife and was in good hands. More than that, being a woman I greatly admired for her strong faith, Julie also knew I had a supportive God and was in even better hands. So, in the big scheme of things, considering that she was instrumental in two major events in my life, I was just glad that if one of the two were going to let me go, it was the bank and not my wife.

CHAPTER 33

Thanks for Your Concern

THERE I was, once again unemployed, with another of life's apparent storms set to come roaring through – but something was different. I had been through storms before and my natural tendency to panic just wasn't present. Having failed miserably at every single job I had tried the past few years maybe I should have been alarmed, but I sensed I was exactly where I was supposed to.

There would be some struggles, which I knew would pass in time, but I would still have to deal with them. My pocketbook was about to take a beating and our finances would be in peril, but we would get through that. Perhaps more of a challenge would be my pride and that feeling of uselessness that would resurface, I knew I would have to work and keep it at bay. Telling my friends that once again I wasn't working would be embarrassing; however, I had done it before and would be able to do it again. None of that was what worried me; rather the toughest part was going to be answering the question people would inevitably ask. What happened? I had no idea what to say and had been asking myself the same thing.

To avoid the discomfort of that conversation, I tried to stay away from crowds and the introvert that I was, being around a lot of people wasn't something I was too keen on anyway. A couple of weeks after being let go I had just come back from spending an hour or so at Riverside Park, the traditional host to Canada Day (July 1st) celebrations in Guelph. There were celebrations throughout the day, followed by what I always considered to be a surprisingly cool fireworks display at night. Sian was doing some fundraising work for the Hospice where she was then working and was keeping the Rotary Club boys in their place at the same time. A large portion of the proceeds of an event they held annually on July 1st were being directed towards her organization. I thought it would be nice to pop by and say hello and then check things out briefly while there.

After arriving and spending a bit of time walking around, I found it funny after realizing that even after eight and half years of sobriety, I had just spent the past half hour or so looking for the 'beer tent'. It wasn't that I had any interest in going in, that's just how conditioned my mind had become over the years. Once I found it, all would be right with the world and I could carry on. If it wasn't there, I wouldn't be able to shake the thought of why in the world people would even want to be there. Maybe I wasn't allowed to drink, but for those that could, what would possess them not to? I still had some work to do on my thinking and was just glad my thoughts weren't transparent – I might get put away just for what ran through my mind.

"Hi Dan, how's the job", of course after hearing my reply, most were sorry they had even asked. I did run into a couple of folks there, as I had over the course of the past couple of weeks. People didn't want a truthful reply when asking a casual question of politeness. "It's awesome", was all they really wanted to hear. In fact that's exactly what I told most of them.

It's also why I stayed away from crowds, as I didn't want them to experience the awkwardness – that and the fact that I couldn't stand small talk to begin with. If I go to a party because there's little choice but to attend, I would feel much better coming out of the night having had one meaningful conversation with one person, than having talked to fifty who walked away thinking of how delighted they were to have met me.

Worse yet, I might be introduced to someone with a friend I ran into, and inevitably one of the first questions that will come of their mouth will be, "so, what do you do for a living?" That's why I wanted to avoid them at the moment. "I'm really not sure" would be about the most honest answer I could give.

Friends I had talked to since leaving my job wanted to know how I was feeling and were genuinely concerned about my future. They knew my story, about the addiction, about my schooling and about why I changed careers. People typically don't get fired on a consistent basis though, and many wondered about the underlying cause. I had talked enough back in the day and told enough stories that I would come up with something to satisfy their curiosity. In reality, their guess was as good as mine.

It reminded me of the days when I would get drunk, more often than not at the worst of all possible times; in front of my parent's friends, before an exam, at my wife's office party, at a wake – too many to count. Those who were closest to me and embarrassed by my behaviour would ask "why in the world would you do such a thing. How could you?"

The feeling now was the same as back then when I would come up with whatever excuse seemed to fit at the time. In reality, their guess as to why I couldn't stop myself from getting drunk at the most inopportune time was as good as mine. In spite of all the great reasons I came up with, the truth was I didn't have the slightest idea – it's just what alcoholics do. This time, I was out of work and didn't know how I got there.

"I'm really sorry to hear about your job … I hope you get back to work soon". That was the most frequent comment and I tried to be appreciative and diplomatic. I also understood that for most people either getting right back into the work force, or at the very least to begin looking at different options, is often the best remedy. It's a sensible way to deal with it – I did neither.

I wanted to spend some time not so much focusing on the storm, rather what could be done to avoid another in the future.

Maybe it wasn't a storm at all. God may very well be trying to send a message and if so, I thought it was more important to pay attention than rush out and pick up work simply for the sake of once more getting fired. It wasn't the neon sign I had wished for, but I might only understand the reason if I came to a stop – completely. It had started with that walk in the forest that next day, a walk in the one place I knew how to shut off everything and listen.

Plenty of others had gone through similar ordeals and I reflected on their stories, some of which I had read and others had heard. One that came to mind was that of Phil Vischer, as told in his book 'Me, Myself and Bob'. He was the creator of the popular kids Veggie Tales series and it is one of the most insightful books I've ever read. As a Christian, with the purest of motives in creating the entire concept as well his company, he couldn't understand where or what God was doing several years later when it all fell apart. Watching an interview on 100 Huntley Street, I would never forget Mr. Vischer's statement, one that managed to put a lot into perspective and amongst the most profound observations I've ever heard.

"I couldn't understand how God could love me so little that He would allow that to happen", he noted in the interview. That's what he felt as everything around him came crashing down. A short time later, in hindsight when he wasn't nearly so entangled in trying to wrestle control, he was able to gain a far clearer picture as to how far off track he had gone and how his ego had been allowed to take control. He was amazed that as he now reflected on the entire ordeal and he wondered "how God could love him so much that He would allow that to happen".

That sounded a lot like the Pierre Burton and Mother Teresa story once again, with a different perception depending on which pair of glasses was being worn. I could relate to that, I had been in the same position many times wondering what in the world God might possibly be up to, only to be grateful later that things had worked the way they did, not as I would have orchestrated it.

A few years earlier as 'the law of attraction' had become so immensely popular, I intentionally ran as far in the other direction as possible from those who tried to preach its virtues. I had nothing against them personally; several good friends in fact had adopted it as a spiritual way of living – they were quite happy. I admired their positive outlook, their drive and ambition – all great qualities and things I needed in my own life. I just knew that for me, the very last thing I needed were for the appetites of my mind to be realized – I might miss out on the very best God had to offer. I don't trust my own thoughts and am far more focused on surrender than on attraction – the two can't coincide in this capacity challenged brain of mine.

CHAPTER 34

The Sweet Sound of Silence

THREE months later, with my kids having just gone back to school, I find myself no closer to a job than the day the door closed behind me and I was told not to come back. It could have been months of frustration and worry, at the end wondering where the time had gone and why I hadn't used it differently. Instead, it was my best summer in years for a variety of reasons, none of which would have unfolded that way had I been working. It wasn't my first experience losing something, only to find as result there's room for something much more important to materialize.

After alcohol had finally beaten me into submission and I received what was a long overdue suspension after pleading guilty to that impaired driving charge, I found myself in a difficult position. Not that I could complain about losing my license, I deserved much worse; it was just going to make it tough to see my kids without having a vehicle. That I could even spend time with my children, I have to give my ex-wife credit. Given the nature of my criminal charge, I was at her mercy and thankful that Nancy had agreed to share custody.

When I did see the kids, our time was spent getting around town by walking or using public transit. I would go to the library and buy a family transit pass and use that to catch a bus downtown, to the mall, to go shopping, or even a take public transit to visit my mom in Oakville. Inevitably, either on a bus or while walking, it lead to a deeper level of conversation than ever experienced in a car. There was never a hurry to get anywhere and the entire point was simply to spend time together. It was relaxed, it was fun, and it was a brand new experience.

Years later, with my license long since reinstated and now living in a house I had purchased (primarily because of my mom's assistance), the kids would at times ask. "Dad, can we get a bus pass this weekend?" They missed that time that was so special together. That lost license was a blessing in disguise, offering us chance to spend time together restoring some of the damage I had caused in the past.

This time, being fired from the bank, I knew there would be plenty to be gained if I avoided focusing on what was lost. Nothing would be gained if went through it kicking and screaming trying to recapture whatever it was that I might have thought I was losing. I wanted to use the time productively and with purpose.

Specifically, I hoped to spend more time with my girls, who now found themselves part of a blended family. It was all new to them, it wasn't easy and I wanted to be available for them. They were getting older and gaining far more independence and with the business that teen years have to offer, there wouldn't be an awful lot of opportunity to do so in the future. The lure of jumping right back into work was there, but this seemed more important.

The timing was impeccable as well, being fired just days before they finished school and their summer break began. Shae Lynn and I spent a lot of time riding bikes through some of the trails just outside of the city. This, the same girl I once resented as a baby because it was her fault that my marriage would remain in shambles and now I got the chance to simply experience the blessing that she was – all because I didn't have a job. Months away herself from becoming a teenager, I was just grateful to have some time together, before she was old enough to realize it wasn't cool to hang out and go biking with her dad.

Amber, an animal lover with several dogs and cats at her mom's house, was now seventeen and lived a full life. She was a little quieter and more reserved than her sister, lacking the same outward confidence – but she had a heart of gold. She was already beyond the point when it was cool to hang out with her dad, but I forged my way in anyway. Even if it was just to spend time taking the dogs on hikes through trails while walking and talking about life. That was something that was needed and this gave me the opportunity to do so.

My kids had never done anything but make me proud and I had a chance to reflect on this during my hiatus. A few years earlier, after listening to a woman from our church speak about a respite program with an organization called 'Christian Horizons', the kids encouraged me to volunteer in that role. It entailed having a child with a disability to spend a weekend a month at the home provider's house, thus giving the child's family a bit of a reprieve, and allow new relationships to form at the same time. I loved the concept, but initially told my daughters the chances were slim. I was a single father, I had a criminal record –there were more suitable candidates to put it mildly. It's one more of those things that kept gnawing at me though and after a few weeks inquired and surprisingly found that they would be delighted to have me.

After a month or two of preliminary work, Justin began to come over and we were thrilled (and still are) to have him for a few days a month. The kids especially, were initially nervous as to what to do and say and how to act, when ultimately what they learned was that Justin just wanted to spend time with them. We didn't have to change anything, just be the family we were and include him in whatever that was – which we did. For me, it was a tremendous opportunity to see my kids engage in a form of behaviour that was completely foreign to what I experienced as a teenager. For a few days a month, they would have to drop whatever immediate needs and desires that seemed so important at the time and actually spend a few days thinking of somebody else. That self centered approach

DAN MATWEY

of 'living everyday like its New Years Eve' and the lack of responsibility that results, was being cut off at its roots, never having the chance to develop – at least not in my backyard. If I did absolutely nothing else for my kids, to be able to model a heart for service at a young age, that perhaps was the most important thing I could do.

Tim has moved to the west coast and after being an intern for a year with an organization that helps inner city kids, he now manages a house and helps new interns in his role as a counsellor. He began after finishing high when he was uncertain what he wanted to do with his life. A year of volunteering in a ministry close to his heart, has given him a firm foundation upon which to build a vocation. His life is anything but that which mine was like when I was the same age. There's no greater delight I find than seeing my kids avoid the same pitfalls that snared me.

I also spent some time with my stepdaughter Cati this summer. Previously living with Sian as a result of her broken marriage, Cati would have her own adjustments to make in this blended marriage. For the most part I got to act as a chauffeur, but there's more to the role than simply driving from point A to point B. It allowed for some barriers to come down and talk about real things. It also gave Cati time to spend with my daughters and see some new relationships begin to flourish. That all would have got lost in the business of what a career brings and never come to fruition had I been working – the more I think about it the more grateful I was to have time off.

I also wanted to have to morning coffee on the front porch with Sian before seeing her off to work. She had taken on a position in a fundraiser role for a local organization she strongly believes in and it's refreshing to see someone approach their job with such enthusiasm – she deserves it. It's her dream job, perfectly matching her skill set and vibrant personality and they're fortunate to have her. It was perfect in our new marriage to spend some time together in the morning, something we otherwise wouldn't have been able to do.

Finally, and one of the greatest blessings as a result of being let go, has been the opportunity to write. I used to love to write, people at work in fact found it quite entertaining. However, I figured any creative juices I once may have possessed had been taken away when I became sober. I used to find it extremely easy to be creative when drinking, granted there would have been more sarcasm and questionable material, but it flowed effortlessly. It's been a long time since I've tried writing seriously and the experience is entirely different.

Without that artificial stimulant to act as a catalyst, I find it at times to be very frustrating. Like every other obstacle I've overcome the past nine years, the only solution is to rely upon God even more – it's where any creativity comes from to begin with. For me, it is simply another level of surrender, one caused by an obstacle. Experience has taught that it always leads to a greater degree of freedom and it's actually pretty cool how God works that way when I think about it. Whatever writing might come as a result almost becomes secondary.

There's one final aspect to touch upon, that being the most important during any period of change I've gone through. What have I learned that I can carry forward and what's the lasting impact of this storm?

CHAPTER 35

Free in Spirit

"Let's go Dan; I've got our next assignment". I could almost hear it coming before rounding the corner and his red pickup truck would soon come into full view stopping at the curb in front of our porch. Behind the wheel was a guy who although he once scared me, I will now tell Sian I miss after going a couple of days without seeing.

Bobby was once one of the city's most notorious drug dealer's during his high school years and a man who lived a lifestyle he's not proud of. He's also not shy to speak about his experience if doing so might benefit someone else. I always thought if there were a modern day St Paul, he would look a lot like Bobby. Formerly, one who used to ridicule the church, God, Christ, you name it – he was now consumed with a passion for ministering to others. Not through preaching, but simply by the manner in which he lived his life. He's spent an inordinate amount of time with the city's homeless; he had an auto body shop for over twenty-five years, the last ten of which had been used to help fix people – not cars. He had been going at a torrid pace and it finally caught up with him and he needed a rest. So he too had the summer off.

I had met Bobby a couple of years ago after attending a Promise Keepers men's conference in Mississauga that fall. It's a Christian event attended by several thousand people and one which attracts quality speakers who address some of the real issues and struggles that men face while trying to live a godly life – it's very real and anything but religious, which appealed to me. A few guys from that Nicaragua trip were going, along with several friends from the Celebrate Recovery program I'm part of. A few things stand out that I distinctly remember about those two days.

Aside from the amazing food and listening to Robin Mark tell stories in his Irish accent before bellowing out any one of his amazing songs, there were also some spectacular speakers. Most had amazing stories, some of which brought them to a pretty low place, but they all have remarkable testimonies about the work God has done in their lives.

Andrew is a good friend from Kortright and another I credit for being instrumental in my journey. I remember telling him as we were listening: "You know, all of these guys have had such tremendous accomplishments. I wish someone would tell a story about how everything went wrong. How they failed at absolutely everything they tried, nonetheless found God right alongside the whole way through". God must have a pretty good sense of humor, because I definitely remember telling Andrew I would like to 'hear' that story – not 'live' it. The other thing I remember was the relentless energy Bobby had put into that weekend trip. Here was a guy who simply wanted others to experience the same joy he had and nothing was going to prevent him from trying.

So he and I spent some time together in the summer, a lot of time. His idea of rest is my idea of going full out – so there was some getting used to. However, I've come to see firsthand what it's like to live 'free in Sprit' – Bobby lives that way. I hadn't met many people who lived without being entangled in something (work, control, investments, relationships), but this was a man who purposely sought that way of life. What I witnessed through one's ability to trust in God to meet his needs, was a greater capacity to serve as result – and Bobby does so with a grateful heart and boldness I'm not accustomed to seeing. This was the freedom I sought.

I think of others who have probably experienced that same

freedom, wondering what it must be like. David for example, that man in a wheelchair I encountered while walking through Parkdale. He was risking all that was comfortable to go back home and simply trusted that God would meet his needs as he abandoned whatever fear would prevent him from going. I also think of several of my own friends from Kortright church. Those ordinary people who helped inspire me to change. People like Kim, who I spent so much time talking to on the sidewalk in front of that small school so many years ago, along with her husband Jim. They're leading a group of teenagers from our church on a trip to Ecuador this winter, a daunting task with a group of teens but which allow them to witness and be part of an awakening that will likely change a lot of lives. They do things like shut down their jobs to spend a week in Haiti after a devastating earthquake and aren't inhibited by the inconvenience of stepping out in faith.

I marvel at Andrew and his wife Anne, who with three young kids amaze me at how radical they'll be in an effort to experience a greater reality through God. There's my good friend Jim from the first Alpha course I took that got me started on this journey. He's a man who is always searching for ways to grow and will never put that responsibility on others by relying on the church, or its many programs to see that happen. I'm always learning something from him just by being in his presence.

My friend Garry comes to mind. To look at him you might think he would strike fear in the heart of any NFL linebacker. Of Ukrainian descent, tall and rough looking, he can be very intimidating. Yet to hear the story's he tells with such humor and sensitivity – a marshmallow might carry more punch. He runs a prison ministry where his own troubled past is used to offer hope to young men incarcerated and uncertain of how to cope with life once they walk out of their prison doors.

I especially admire some younger people I'm fortunate enough to know, those who live a life so immensely different than what I did at their age. Rachel and Amy especially come to mind, a couple of beautiful and extremely gifted young ladies. One has a rare ability to teach kids and teenagers, along with heart for orphans that she doesn't hesitate to act on. The other simply wants to give back to God with the talents she has been blessed with in her ability to sing and write music. They're far removed from conforming to the patterns of the world, particularly at an age where there's so much pressure to do so. I can only hope and pray that my own daughters might grow up as young women to be just like them.

I look at these friends, or many others I admire, and find it interesting that none are wealthy. Nor are they driven by success – by world standards they would be considered quite ordinary. Yet they've found a richness most people wouldn't even believe could exist. They're my hero's today, individuals who actually embody the lifestyle that Rick Warren talked about in his book The Purpose Driven Life.[5]

Right now I could only aspire to achieve what they have, but I also have a future that I'm very uncertain about – there's hope in that. I'm acutely aware of the fact that most of what I've done in terms of my career has been anything but fruitful, so the truth is I haven't really lost an awful lot by being fired. I'm grateful God sees me as being important enough to intervene to help me see it that way. I'm even beginning to believe that this most unlikely path I've taken is for one simple reason – He must want so much more from me. In the meantime, until that neon sign appears, I'll keep on trying and if I fall, get back up, persevere, and do it all over again. After failing enough times, there really is profound freedom that's resulted from it.

Right now I'm running on empty, which is precisely where I like it. I'm going to get filled with something, and as long as it's not my own selfish ambitions that are the driving force, there's a good

---

5 Warren, Rick. The Purpose Driven Life (Michigan, Zondevan Publishing, 2002).

chance one day I'll experience a reality unlike one I've even known – maybe even something to write about.

Finally, and perhaps the person I most admire and I believe found a 'freedom of spirit' most mortals could barely comprehend, is Mother Teresa. After a mystical experience and a conversation with Christ during a train ride in India, she set forth on a lifelong vocation that overcame every obstacle it encountered – including an extended period of darkness.[6] She may very well have achieved a level of intimacy and connection to God that most of us couldn't imagine possible. One of my favorite prayers is one that was written on the wall of her humble home in Calcutta. To my knowledge, Mother Teresa was never an addict of any sort, but as someone who spent the better part of my life paralyzed by fear and my relationships to others, I don't know of any words that better capture what my ultimate goal might be today. Any time I share my story I'll end with this prayer, so it only seems appropriate to do so here. If you've never seen this before, I hope you take the time to fully absorb the full implications of these words. God bless you on your own journey.

---

6 Kolodiejchuk, Brian, ed. *Mother Teresa: Come Be My Light* (New York, Doubleday Publishing 2007) Pg 39

The Final Analysis

People are often unreasonable, illogical, and self-centered;
... Forgive them anyway!

If you are kind, people may accuse you of selfish, ulterior motives;
... Be kind anyway!

If you are successful, you will win some false friends and some true enemies;
... Succeed anyway!

If you are honest and frank, people may cheat you;
... Be honest and frank anyway!

What you spend years building, someone could destroy overnight;
... Build anyway!

If you find serenity and happiness, they may be jealous;
... Be happy anyway!

The good you do today, people will often forget tomorrow;
... Do good anyway!

Give the world the best you have, and it may never be enough;
... Give the world the best you've got anyway!

You see, in the final analysis, it is between you and God;
... It was never between you and them... anyway

ABOUT THE AUTHOR

Dan, along with his wife Sian, lives in Guelph, Ontario. After getting married on New Year's Eve 2010, they now share what some refer to as a Brady Bunch family. Dan has a son and two daughters, and Sian two sons and a daughter herself. Having been on their own and raising kids for the past nine years, there's both a strong degree of support and encouragement in seeing one another try to fulfill their dreams, along with a fair amount of independence in maintaining the strong foundation they've each built over that period of time.

Dan has an MBA from Wilfred Laurier University, a program in which he enrolled in 2003 at the age of 43. Having spent 20 years prior to that working in the manufacturing sector, he was unexpectedly let go from that position several months into his journey of recovery. Thus began the process of finding a new career. To help facilitate that goal while moving into the financial services industry, Dan has achieved the designation as a Certified Financial Planner. In light of his own family experience, along with a heartfelt desire to contribute something he felt was lacking in financial planning, Dan made it a commitment to specialize in helping families affected by disability. There's enough emotional turbulence as it is, financial uncertainty need not, and doesn't have to be, added to that. That continues to be his dream and one he looks to with eager anticipation to see fulfilled one day. The unlikely road to get there was the motivating factor that inspired him to write his first book.

Email the author: dan@testimonyontap.com